ADVENTURE AT NAMELESS VALLEY RANCH

Sharon R. Todd

ADVENTURE AT NAMELESS VALLEY RANCH

Review and Herald Publishing Association
Washington, D.C.

Editor: Bobbie Jane Van Dolson
Book Design: Kaaren Kinzer
Cover and Inside Illustrations: Bobbi Tull

Library of Congress Cataloging in Publication Data
81-162

ISBN 0-8280-0032-8

Printed in U.S.A.

Dedicated to
Helen, Joe, Lloyd,
Tony, Rosalea, and Esther,
whose lively adventures
are a never-failing source
of story material.

Contents

1

Arrival

Dust kicked up behind the blue station wagon as the Browns turned off the farm road into the ranch property. A large stone obelisk indicating that the camp belonged to the Texas Conference of Seventh-day Adventists greeted them as they bumped along the rough road over the open grounds of the ranch.

"Where do we go to register Helen?" Mother held 3-year-old Rosie more tightly and glanced anxiously about for signs of life. The ranger's house and several trailers stood near the entrance, but there were no markers to guide campers.

Father motioned toward the left. "Probably up there at the cabins."

The seven Browns had not been to Nameless Valley Ranch in almost a year. At that time only one or two unfinished cabins marked the spot where actual construction had begun. Now there were new-looking buildings, both finished and unfinished, everywhere. Mother nodded in agreement. The cabins did seem the most likely place to begin looking. She had heard that the cafeteria was completed, as well as some of the other buildings. Now they would get to see them.

"I don't remember this road's being so narrow." Mother sounded a bit nervous as she peered across the road to a rather sheer drop-off on the driver's side. "It wouldn't do to meet anyone coming down this hill."

But just as they rounded the next curve, they were greeted by a puff of dust and the grinding of gears. "Oh, no!" Mother groaned softly.

"This is fun," said 5-year-old Timmy happily.

Father pulled as far as he could to his side of the road and waited for the oncoming pickup to pass. But the other driver, feeling it was safer where he waited, motioned for the station wagon to come on, so Father gingerly squeezed past the pickup. Helen, crowded among her brothers in the back seat, heard small shrubs scraping the car as they eased through.

"Whew!" Everyone let out their breath at once and laughed.

"I wouldn't want to do that every day," Father chuckled.

The station wagon pulled steadily up the curving hill until several unfinished cabins came into sight.

"We're here!" Helen shouted. "Here!" echoed Rosie, and the three boys strained to see the horses, but none were in view.

The station wagon continued to move slowly along. At the cabins, a handful of workers glanced at the carful of Browns. No one else was in sight.

"There's the cafeteria!" Joe yelled as they rounded the last curve and came to a large clearing. Several cars were parked in a group near a long, low building made of stone.

"I guess that's it." Father got out and stretched his legs before crossing to the building, where he saw a few people walking around.

In a few minutes he was back, motioning for the family to come. The children piled out eagerly and ran toward the cafeteria. Mother followed more slowly.

"Hello, hello." The youth director's broad grin welcomed them. "Come on in. Right over there to register." He motioned to the other end of the building, where several tables were pushed together. Behind them sat two or three men and women apparently handling all the details of registration.

"Hello, Helen, Bill, Susan. Long time no see!" The youthful man with the wavy hair and old-fashioned mustache greeted them

10

cheerfully from his post behind the first table.

"Pastor Don! We just saw you last Sabbath!" Helen protested, and the pastor grinned at her.

"Is this where Helen registers?" Mother asked, smiling. She was relieved to know that her daughter would have a friend right from the beginning.

Pastor Don nodded, and the Browns took their place in line and followed the others down the row of tables. First the cashier, then the nurse.

"How's Helen feeling?" Doryne, Pastor Don's attractive wife, asked in her most professional manner.

"Excited," Mother returned with a pleasant laugh.

"Are you working here too, Mrs. Layton?" Helen asked. She had great admiration for the pastor's wife.

"Yes, Helen, I'm the nurse and the girls' director."

Helen smiled at the young woman's soft English accent. "Great!"

At the next table, the Browns looked over the list of activities available. "What are some of the things you want to do while you are here at NVR this week?" the youthful male counselor asked with a broad grin.

"Horseback riding and swimming—and crafts," Helen added quickly.

"When do you want to swim, in the morning or afternoon?"

Mother and daughter held a short conference, then Helen chirped, "Afternoon, I guess."

"Fine." The young man made a note of Helen's name, and the Browns moved on to "Cabin Assignments."

"You'll be in the Pharr Cabin." The young lady at this table drew a quick map for them.

"With a name like that it sounds as if it ought to be miles away." Mother teased Helen lightly, her eyes twinkling at her daughter's excitement.

"Shall we go find the cabin now, and then drive around to the old creek for a swim?'' Father asked as the family regrouped by the car.

The boys were all for a swim right away, but Helen wanted to see the cabin first. Mother settled it by saying they would do it Helen's way, since she was the one going to camp. So Father backed the car from the level clearing and cautiously guided it over ruts left by the heavy machinery. He gingerly turned onto the path that would take them in back of the garage that served as a kitchen and then on up the hill to the girls' cabins.

"She said it's the third one on the right, counting the foundation.'' Mother studied the instructions, then the surroundings, to be sure of her bearings.

"There's the first cabin.'' Helen pointed to a small wooden building, freshly built, but with no door or windows yet in place.

The road grew even rougher as Father slowed the car to a crawl.

"Here's the foundation." A gray slab stood bare and expectant. A future cabin to be erected soon.

"It must be right up ahead," Mother added hopefully.

But Father had halted the car.

"It doesn't look as though we're going to be able to drive to it, for there's no more road. Only ruts and gravel."

So again the family piled out of the car and struggled to follow Father along the rough path that led, they hoped, to the Pharr Cabin. "Maybe that's a good name for it after all," Mother muttered softly.

Picking their way across a gutter that lay open waiting for a large pipe, they arrived at the cabin, an almost exact replica of the one they had seen at the foot of the hill. Mother, Father, and the five children stared solemnly at the small wooden building, doorless and windowless.

A cheerful, round, sun-tanned face popped through a window space. "Hello! Come on in!"

"We're trying to," Father called back.

The boys began to chase a frog that caught their eye, and Rosie slipped and fell into a mound of dirt. Mother picked her up and dusted her off, but the child couldn't keep her footing. Finally Father scooped her up in one arm, and carrying the suitcase in the other hand, he crossed the open gutter to the "porch" of the cabin in two large steps.

"Well, we made it." Mother's breath came quickly for a moment as she stood in the center of the open room and surveyed the cabin that her older daughter would call home for the next week.

Helen looked around too, and for the first time felt uncertain about camp. The building seemed more like a skeleton than a cabin. Completely unfinished on the inside, with only exposed studs showing where the two main rooms, bathroom, and closets would be, it appeared rather strange and uninviting.

"You should have seen it a few days ago," Darci, the round-faced counselor, added pleasantly. "They've really done a lot to it. They'll have it finished sometime in the next couple of weeks."

Helen said nothing, but she lugged her suitcase to the second large room and laid it beside one of the four mattresses that spread along the walls like wagon spokes.

"They'll get the beds in later. For now we're roughing it," Darci explained quickly.

A large water cooler sat in one corner, and a shower stall rested near its final destination. But no toilets were in sight.

"Where do you go to the bathroom?" Mother couldn't resist asking.

Darci pointed to a blue "porta-potty" just beyond the cabin.

Mother laughed and ruffled Helen's hair. "Well, hon, it looks as though roughing it is exactly what you'll be doing."

Helen grinned in silence. She hardly knew what to think of it all. Since this was to be her first time at camp and everything was so new to her, she hadn't really known *what* to expect.

The three boys exploded through the doorway. "Can we go swimming now?"

"Is it OK if we take Helen with us for a while?" Mother asked the counselor.

Darci nodded. "Lunch is at twelve-thirty. You can meet the other counselor then. Her name is Tammy."

It was only eleven by Helen's watch. "We have plenty of time," she said. She was feeling happier now.

Running and stumbling over the rough ground, the boys reached the car first. A fine coat of dust had settled on Lonnie's jeans where he had fallen on the path.

Mother hardly spoke as Father eased the station wagon cautiously back down the long, curving grade to the main road. At the bottom of the hill she sighed and looked relieved until Lonnie spoke up brightly. "We have to go up and down that road again today."

"Horses!" yelled Joe. And sure enough, near where the family had turned off the main road to head up the hill several grown horses and a few colts peered over the rails of a small corral.

"Are they the ones you're going to ride?" Timmy asked eagerly.

"I don't know." Helen studied the penned horses. "But a couple sure are pretty."

The road curved around a large fenced area where a few cows and several more horses grazed, and then it stretched out between the pasture and the creek for several hundred yards. Picking his way carefully, Father drove the length of the road as far as it went.

"There's the place we camped last summer," Joe informed his younger brothers, who had not been with the family on that particular trip.

"Can we go swimming?"

"Can we?"

Father held up a hand for silence. "Yes, but stay right here in the shallow part where we can see you."

The water was not actually deep enough for swimming, but the boys enthusiastically splashed and tossed small pebbles.

Helen wandered a little way down the creek. She remembered the camping trip the summer before, when they had lain out under the stars, roasted "hot dogs," sat by the campfire singing and talking until late at night, and climbed their "mountain." It had been nice to be out here then. "Surely camp will be as much fun as that was," she whispered softly.

"Helen!" Father's voice brought her quickly back to the present.

"Coming!" she called and hurried to the car.

"They all got back into their places, and the faithful station wagon safely climbed the dangerous hill for the second time. Father parked in the clearing.

A large group of people had already gathered for lunch, and the Browns paid for their meal and joined them.

"This is pretty good." Helen ate quickly. She was surprised at her appetite.

"I hope you enjoy all your meals this much. Maybe we'll get some meat on our skinny daughter." Mother playfully offered Helen her own plate.

Later there were goodbyes and kisses and promises to write. A

15

cloud of dust swirled up from the back of the station wagon as the car turned out of sight on its way down the hill for the last time that day. "I hope they make it back all right," Helen said aloud. In the silence that followed, she felt a small lump in her throat.

"Come on, Helen," Darci called out as she passed. "Meet some of your cabin mates."

A tiny blonde girl about a foot shorter than Helen stood to one side. She looked lost and frightened.

"Prissy, meet Helen. She's in our cabin, and this is her first time at camp too."

"Hello." Prissy's voice was soft and unsure.

"Have you eaten yet, Prissy?" the counselor asked.

"No . . . I didn't know what to do."

"Well, you get in line, take a plate, and when it is your turn just tell the people which things you want, and they'll dish them out. Real simple." Darci put an arm around the girl's shoulders. "Come on, I'll show you this time, and you'll know how." The counselor stopped and turned to Helen. "You've eaten, haven't you?"

"Sure." Helen nodded. "Can I go on up to the cabin now?"

"Yes. I think Tammy has a couple more new girls up there. You can meet them, too."

Helen picked her way carefully back up the path. Sliding once, she caught herself before she fell. Roughing it is right, she thought.

"You made it back all in one piece." Tammy greeted her and pretended to be surprised. Pointing behind her, she added, "We have three more roommates." Turning to a red-headed girl about Helen's height, she introduced her first. "Helen, this is Ginger. This is her first time at camp too."

Ginger said nothing, but she looked sharply at Helen, then turned her back and continued to unpack her suitcase.

"Hello," Helen offered hopefully.

But Ginger only slammed the lid down on the suitcase and dropped to the mattress with her back to everyone.

Tammy frowned, then turned to two girls, both freckled and

16

blonde, obviously twins. Sitting crosslegged on the mattresses they had pushed together, their mouths hung open as they stared at Ginger.

"Helen, these are the twins, Susie and Lucy. They said everyone at home just calls them the twins."

Susie and Lucy giggled and chorused, "Hello."

"They're first-timers too."

After a warm greeting for the twins, Helen crossed to the second room, where she would be sleeping. None of the girls on her side were in the cabin, but two suitcases stood open by the mattresses opposite her own. What would her roommates be like? Surely not like Ginger. But what if they were?

With free time on her hands, Helen made up her bed, then stretched out to finish reading the book she had begun on the way to camp. She had read just a page or two when soft music from the front room caught her attention, and laying the book aside, she joined Darci and Tammy as they listened to Linda from Unit Three playing the flute. A gnawing in her stomach made Helen eager to head for the cafeteria when the counselors called suppertime, but her steps were heavier as she returned to the cabin later. The gnawing remained.

"Food is rotten here!" The voice was sharp and unexpected. Ginger tossed her red hair back over her shoulder. "Look at this dumb cabin. You can't even see. There's no lights."

"We should have electricity in a couple of days," Darci commented mildly.

"We have our flashlights in the meantime," Tammy added.

"Let's get ready for campfire." Darci pulled out her flashlight and lined up the girls. "Dawn and Marge, meet Helen, Prissy, the twins, and Ginger." Everyone smiled and said Hello—except Ginger, who sighed impatiently.

"I hope the bugs don't eat us alive" was this delightful girl's only comment as the group started down the path to campfire.

Helen followed behind Darci and Tammy and tried to help Prissy, who kept sliding and stumbling in her slick-soled shoes.

"Look out, Clumsy," Ginger snapped as Prissy fell. "Why

didn't you wear tennis shoes?''

Tears sprang to Prissy's eyes. Ginger pushed past roughly and quickly disappeared in the dusk.

Helen glared after her as she helped Prissy to her feet.

''I sure hope she's in a better mood tomorrow,'' Helen muttered.

''Me too,'' Prissy whispered softly.

Hurrying as quickly as they could, the two girls caught up with their cabin mates.

After the campfire they returned to their cabin and undressed for bed in the dark.

Someone tripped over a suitcase, and Ginger's sharp voice let out a yell.

Helen couldn't resist a smile. She would not let anyone or anything spoil her stay at NVR. As she lay staring into the darkness, thoughts of horseback riding, swimming, and canoeing all raced through her mind, followed by visions of interesting crafts, and she wondered whether morning would ever come.

2
Night Visitor

Muffled laughter broke into Helen's sleep. Through one slightly opened eye she saw Dawn and Marge chatting quietly as they sat in their pajamas on their mattresses. Helen stretched and sat up.

"It was so dark I almost couldn't find my shoes or a flashlight. I didn't think I was going to make it outside to the bathroom." Dawn giggled, and her face flushed.

"Did you?" Marge asked in mock seriousness.

"Yes!" Dawn yelped and struck her friend with her pillow.

Just as they began a good pillow fight Prissy let out a shriek. Darci jumped out of bed and tumbled over to the little girl's mattress.

"There's something in my shoe," Prissy whimpered pitifully.

Darci retrieved the shoe from the middle of the room where Prissy had slung it. She turned it upside down and dumped out a three-inch, turned-up-tail insect. "It's a scorpion," she told the frightened girl. With a sound thud she brought the shoe down on the offending creature. Taking a tissue from under her pillow, Darci scooped up the remains and tossed the whole thing in the garbage sack.

"All gone." Darci stretched tall and then fell heavily onto her mattress.

"We had lots of those at camp last year," Marge injected matter-of-factly.

"This isn't your first year at camp?" Helen asked the brown-haired, slightly plump girl who squinted back through thick

19

glasses and managed to look pleasant in spite of them.

"Naw. My third. I've been going to camp since I was 8. Next year I'll be going to junior camp."

Helen studied her two roommates. "Are you sisters?"

Dawn giggled again. "No, but everyone at church says we should be."

"My mom keeps threatening to ship me off to Dawn's house."

"And my mom says she's going to send me to Marge's."

"So far, neither one of them has done it though!"

"It doesn't sound as though you two would mind living together."

"Actually, I can't stand the kid," Marge said in that dry way that was her special gift. "That's why I pick on her so much." And with that she resumed the interrupted attack with her pillow amid laughter and tickling.

"All right, guys, get up and get dressed," Tammy yelled over the growing noise.

A joint protest arose from the mattresses where the twins lay barely stirring. Their feet dangling over the ends invited a tickle from Tammy that brought both sleepy girls suddenly upright.

"Get with it, lazyheads."

Making up the beds, or rather the mattresses, was easy if you didn't mind doing it on your knees, Helen thought as she crawled around on the floor. She dressed quickly in shorts. The day already promised to be warm.

"Oh, yes," Darci called out, "those of you who are riding horses in the morning have to wear long pants now. If you're riding in the afternoon put on your long pants after lunch. *No one* is allowed to ride unless she has on long pants."

Groaning softly, Helen changed to her jeans.

"That's the stupidest rule I've heard so far," Ginger muttered angrily. It was her first remark of the day. "I've ridden horses lots of times in shorts."

Darci, busy helping Prissy make up her bed, turned slowly to

Ginger and repeated simply, "No long pants, no ride. It's your choice."

Still grumbling, Ginger slipped into her jeans and slammed her suitcase shut. As soon as morning devotional ended she jumped up and walked toward the door of the cabin, tossing her Bible carelessly on the mattress as she passed.

"Ginger!" Marge called out.

The redhead turned on her heels. The expression on her face was a challenge.

"You didn't make up your bed."

"I don't have to."

"That's another rule at camp," Darci announced in a no-nonsense tone.

As Ginger started out the door the second time Tammy stepped in her way. "No breakfast until that bed is made." Her voice was low and pleasant, but she definitely meant business.

"No great loss," Ginger muttered. "The food stinks anyway."

Tammy stood firm, and Ginger finally backed down enough to recross the room and go through the motions of making her bed. But the rumpled sheets she left behind as she started out the cabin for the third time left a great deal to be desired.

Darci sighed heavily and turned from helping Prissy rearrange her Bible, flashlight, and suitcase, to smooth out the sheets on Ginger's mattress.

Marge, Dawn, and Helen stood for a moment watching the counselor in silence.

"Man, I wouldn't put up with that a minute," Marge informed Helen as they finally picked their way down the hill for general line call.

"If she's so miserable here why in the world did she come, I wonder," Helen mused as they lined up in the clearing near the cafeteria.

"Beats me," Marge muttered back.

After Pledge and roll call Helen's cabin led out for the breakfast line. Later they regrouped at the cabin for their towels and everything else they would need until lunchtime. Then they returned to the clearing and boarded the bus that would take them to the swimming hole and the corral.

"I hope I get a tame horse," Helen whispered a bit anxiously to Marge.

"Last year I got one so tame he went to sleep every time I got on him," Marge answered dryly.

Helen exploded in a giggle and laughed so hard she almost fell off the back seat of the bus. Too bad Ginger isn't as nice as Marge, she thought ruefully.

The bus stopped first at the pond halfway down the "big hill," as the girls dubbed it, to let off the swimmers, then meandered down to the main road, where it turned left.

"Is this all the horses they have?" Ginger asked in apparent shock as the campers piled out by the little corral the Browns had passed the day before.

"There's lots more over there." Helen motioned to the large pasture where cattle grazed lazily. No other horses were in sight at the moment, and Ginger raised her eyebrows questioningly before heading for the corral.

A slender girl with long black hair stepped over to the group and smiled broadly. She was wearing a plaid shirt, jeans, and boots, and she wore a ten-gallon hat. "Here in Texas you're expected to greet people with a big Howdy, so I reckon I'll go along with that. Howdy! I'm Julie!"

"Howdy!" chorused most of the expectant boys and girls.

"How many of you have never ridden before?" The girl counted hands. "H'mmm, not too bad. Seem to have a lot of experienced folk here today. Afraid you're going to find this first lesson a bit dry, but we'll just think of it as a limbering-up exercise before the real thing."

An equally slender boy in matching jeans, shirt, boots, and hat stepped up with a large box full of brushes.

"This here is Pete. He's my sidekick. He's going to pass out the brushes while I show you the fine art of currying a horse.''

Ginger's sighs were audible and frequent during the short demonstration on proper brushing of the horses.

"Since some of our audience seem a bit impatient, Pete, why don't we set 'em right to it.''

Ginger jumped off the fence where she had been watching the demonstration, grabbed a brush, and strode over to a large black-and-brown beauty whose coat she began to brush with a rather heavy stroke.

"Yowl!" Ginger threw down the brush and backed off, rubbing at her left shoulder. "That horse bit me!''

Julie grinned broadly as she snuggled the horse and fondly rubbed his nose. "This horse is Dandy. And he don't cotton to rough handling.'' Her eyes twinkled as she handed the brush back to Ginger. "I'd suggest a slightly lighter touch next time.''

Helen's horse, a gray-and-white mare with long black mane, nibbled contentedly at the leaves of the tree within her reach as Helen gently rubbed her sides with the brush. It was fun watching the mare's coat begin to shine, and she was surprised to hear Julie's voice announce the end of the class.

Hands on hips, Ginger faced the cowgirl. "Aren't we going to ride them?''

"That comes tomorrow—after we teach you how to saddle 'em.''

Ginger turned away with a loud "humph" and angrily boarded the bus. "If I'd known that, I would have worn shorts anyway.''

Helen, Marge, and Dawn made their way to the back seat of the bus. They were purposely getting as far from Ginger as possible.

"I wonder if anyone has ever drowned in the swimming hole?'' Marge asked quietly.

"Don't you know how to swim?'' Helen whispered back.

"Sure she does!'' Dawn exclaimed, surprised at Marge's question.

"Oh, I wasn't thinking about me.'' Marge's squinty gaze was fixed on the back of the unfriendly redhead.

"Marge!" Helen gasped and then collapsed in giggles.

A broad grin covered the girl's face. "I was only kidding."

Dawn and Helen grabbed the chubby girl and tickled her until Marge cried, "Uncle."

"Swimming hole. Everybody off," Peaches announced over the noise. Helen wasn't sure what the bus driver's real name was; everyone just liked to call him Peaches.

"I was supposed to swim in the afternoon," said Helen, "but here I go!" She stripped off the jeans and shirt that covered her swimsuit and threw her clothes to one side. "Yuck!" She grimaced as she stepped into the water and felt the murky bottom.

"I think they're filling in the pond with sand." Marge motioned to large piles of sand and light gravel nearby.

"Boy, does it need it!" Dawn stepped daintily into the water for a few feet then struck out in a smooth breast stroke.

"She sure isn't afraid of the water." Helen admired the younger girl as Dawn performed a series of difficult strokes, then returned to the beach. "That was great. You sure can swim."

"Beats riding horses." The younger girl beamed. "This pond would be nice if it weren't for the bottom."

"How come you're taking horseback riding if you don't like it?"

"It's my mom's idea. She thinks it will be good for me."

"Dawn's afraid of falling off a horse," Marge explained as the younger girl headed back out to the water. "What she really wants to do is swim. She'd make a great duck. She's going to get web feet if she keeps it up."

None too soon for Helen, the bus could be heard chugging up the hill from the horse corral, and the counselor whistled for everyone to get dressed and reboard.

Vainly trying to dry off, Helen tugged her jeans and shirt over the wet suit and slipped into her tennis shoes.

"I'm sure glad I didn't pick swimming first and *then* horseback riding," Marge muttered as she struggled into her jeans.

"Can you imagine squishing along on the horses!" Dawn

24

laughed so hard she could hardly pull her shirt over her head.

The three girls again grabbed the back seat and tried to hang on as the bus hit every bump in the road. Their wet jeans made them slide off the seat with every jolt. Laughing until they could hardly stand it, they "squished" up the path to the cabin and stripped off the wet clothes.

"Move it!" Darci called as everyone dressed. "Time for village line call and lunch."

After lining up in front of the cabin for a quick roll call, the girls hurried to the lunch line. They forgot all about Ginger, as they wolfed down their meal and took advantage of the short free time to see what the camp store had to offer.

Later, the girls returned to their cabin.

"You have a half hour for quiet talk or rest, or reading, or whatever," announced Tammy.

Helen stretched out on her mattress and folded her hands behind her head. The book she had tucked into her suitcase beckoned her, but the effort seemed too much. "Hey, Marge, what do you think we'll do after quiet time?" A yawn overtook her as she finished the sentence. Helen didn't hear her friends answer as she began to breathe slowly and evenly.

Helen felt someone shaking her shoulder, and frowned as she tried to pull away and turn over.

"Up and at it." Darci's voice reached down through the fog and lifted the girl back to consciousness.

"Is quiet time over already?"

"For you it was more like nap time."

Helen stretched and sat up.

All the girls were piling out of the cabin. "What now?" Helen asked with another yawn.

"Surprise time. Every day after quiet time we'll have a surprise."

Helen liked surprises, so she jumped to her feet and scampered after her cabin mates.

25

"Today we have two items on the agenda," announced the director. "First, camp development, followed by a nature walk."

The girls of unit one followed Darci and Tammy to a predesignated spot.

"We are in charge of all this area in front of the cafeteria and cook's garage." Darci waved an arm to indicate their territory. "Pick up all the sticks, trash, and other inappropriate items and toss them over there." Her left arm pointed to a large receptacle by the cook's garage marked "TRASH."

"I think we've been suckered into a cleanup detail," observed Marge with a grin.

In just a few minutes Helen's back ached from the bending and stooping, and the whistle didn't seem to blow soon enough for her.

The nature walk took them up a path past the cafeteria and over a hill, up another hill, and down again. Rounding a bend, Helen let out a giggle. "I know where we are!"

Marge raised an eyebrow.

"We camped here last year—my family and I."

After exploring the area for a while, Darci pointed out a natural grapevine swing that the Browns had not noticed. Tucking up her legs, Helen attempted the swing. "My 3-year-old sister would love this."

All too soon the counselors gave the signal to return. Retracing their steps, the group started back for the camp to prepare for supper. Catching her foot on something, Helen stopped short. Bending to examine what had tripped her, she tugged at the slightly embedded item until it gave way. Holding it up high, Helen tried to whistle. "Hey, gang!" she finally called. Marge, Dawn, and Darci, trailing behind the others, were the first to reach her.

"Wow!"

"Let me see that."

"Is it real?" Dawn's voice sounded faint as she gingerly touched the shell Helen held out for them to examine. Approximately 6 inches in diameter, it was the largest snail shell any of them had ever seen.

26

"Bring it back to the cabin," Darci suggested. "That will be something to take home as a souvenir."

So Helen hurried back to the cabin, clutching the fossilized snail shell. She could hardly wait to show Tammy and the twins.

"Aren't you lucky?" the twins chorused. They had been hunting for unusual bugs, rocks—anything—since their arrival.

"Would you like to have it?" Helen held it out to the tow-headed girls. They glanced first at each other and then at Helen, then shook their heads.

"No, you found it."

Helen wrapped it carefully in some soft underwear and tucked it in a safe corner of her suitcase. She could hardly wait to show it to her class at church school next year.

Clean clothes felt good as Helen changed for supper. General line call was brief, and in the cafeteria she took a generous share of everything offered, but the food couldn't ease the gnawing in her stomach.

"Don't you like the food?" Marge noticed Helen's half-full plate as her friend tossed the remains in the trash can.

"Ginger's right about one thing. The food really isn't as good as my mom's cooking. Except breakfast. I'm going to starve."

Marge's eyebrows shot up as she glanced at Helen's very slender figure.

"Don't do that! They might move Ginger to your bed, and that would put her next to me."

Helen couldn't resist laughing at the idea of Ginger putting up with Dawn and Marge's giggles and whispering, not to mention their daily pillow fights.

The girls raced back to the cabin. "I can hardly wait for campfire. That's my favorite part, I think—next to the horses." Helen was breathless, but she still managed to talk.

"I wonder if they'll put on skits this year." Marge puffed as she tried to match Helen's long-legged strides. "I really enjoyed them at the camp I went to last year."

Armed with their flashlights, the girls formed a line and retraced the path they had taken earlier on the nature walk. At the top of the first hill they veered to the left into a large clearing. In the center of this open space the boys had built a huge tepee-style campfire that had just begun to blaze nicely.

As darkness began to settle around the assembled campers, a short, slightly stocky young woman stepped to the clearing and began to strum on her guitar. "All right, what'll we sing first?"

"'Side by Side,'" shouted one camper.

"'Pass It On,'" called out another group.

Several more voices vied for attention.

"Hold it! Hold it! One at a time." Strumming a few chords she suggested, "Let's start with 'Pass It On.'"

The campers' voices were raised in song after song as Debbie, the guitarist, led out.

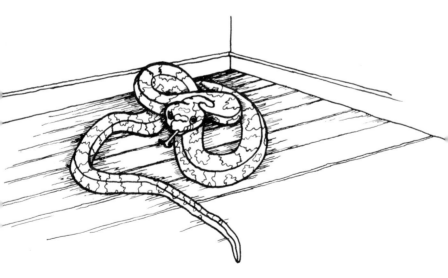

Helen glanced over at Ginger, who sat staring into the fire. Not once did she see Ginger join in. ''I wonder if she doesn't like to sing.'' Helen shrugged and raised her hand to suggest a song.

All too soon the music, the talk by Pastor Jack, and prayer were all over, and the girls wearily made their way to their cabin, where they undressed in the dark.

It had been a long, busy day, and silence soon settled over the cabin as one by one the tired campers dozed off.

Suddenly a scream pierced the darkness, and Helen sat upright in bed.

The eerie light from two flashlights made a small pathway from the counselors' beds to the twins, who had let out the yell.

''What is it?'' The muffled voices of the counselors could be heard as they knelt by Lucy and Susie.

Helen heard the word *snake* and quickly drew her feet up under her. Grabbing her own flashlight from under her pillow, she shined it around her mattress, but nothing unusual caught her eye.

One by one the girls woke up and switched on their flashlights. Excited voices filled the cabin as Darci and Tammy moved some spare mattresses that had been standing against the wall in the corner.

''There it is!'' Prissy yelled and tore across the cabin to the room where Helen, Marge, and Dawn sat cowering on their beds.

All the girls began to scream as the counselors tried to reach the snake with a broom.

''Is it a rattler?'' Tammy murmured softly to Darci. But the girls only heard the word *rattler* and yelled again.

A masculine voice at the door of the cabin quieted them as the youth director asked what seemed to be the matter.

''There's a snake in here. I've got it cornered, I think.'' Darci sounded relieved.

Taking the broom Darci offered, the director managed to lift the snake from its hiding place and carry it safely away from the cabin.

''Was it a rattler?'' the girls chorused as the director returned.

''No, just a harmless rat snake,'' he announced with a grin. ''If

29

you have any more visitors tonight, let me know.'' Waving to the girls, the director disappeared into the dark.

One by one the girls calmed down enough to turn off their flashlights and lie down. But quiet was not completely restored for some time.

Helen had almost drifted off to sleep again when her eyes popped open. A frown creased her brow. ''I didn't do any crafts today. I know it was on my list.'' She tried to recall whether the counselor who had signed her up for the activities had said anything about crafts' just being some days and not every day. ''Oh, well.'' She yawned and turned over. ''Maybe tomorrow.''

3
Surprises

Moving day! Rise and shine!'' Tammy's strong voice broke off the remaining edges of sleep, and Helen opened heavy eyelids to watch the counselors as they packed up their suitcases and prepared to go someplace.

"Where are we moving?" The twins, eager for a new adventure, hopped up and began gathering their things together.

"Our new cabin," Darci announced triumphantly. "We're moving up in the world."

The cabin turned out to be down the hill, not up, but the girls ohed and ahed as they entered. It had a door and windows, was finished on the inside, and looked more like a real cabin.

"There's a shower!" Dawn called in glee.

"And a regular toilet!" Helen could remember hunting for *her* shoes and flashlight in the middle of the night.

Ginger flipped the switch by the door. "I should have known it was too good to be true," she muttered when the lights remained unlit.

"Oh, well, look at all the things we *do* have." The twins raced from the first room to the second room and back again. "We even have a closet."

Tammy huffed and puffed as she lugged in the large red-and-white water cooler. "But we *don't* have running water—unless I trip down the hill with this thing."

The girls laughed as they tried to picture Tammy racing down the hill lugging the water cooler; then they set about admiring the cabin some more.

"Devotional, cabin cleanup, breakfast call!" Darci clapped her hands to restore order.

"We don't want to fall down on our points in our new cabin. So far we have a perfect ten points Sunday and Monday for cabin inspection. Let's not slack off now."

"No way!" Helen called out as she grabbed her Bible and joined the girls in the first room.

After devotional the girls fell to making their beds and arranging the flashlight and Bible on their pillows, with the suitcases just so at the foot of the mattresses and extra suitcases neatly to one side.

"Ginger can sweep inside, Helen clean the windows, and Prissy check out the bathroom. The twins can take care of trash, and Dawn and Marge can sweep the porch."

Ginger reluctantly took the broom Darci offered and began to sweep the wood floor of the cabin. Small dust clouds rose up as she swished the broom back and forth. The harder she swept, the more clouds rose until the room began to look hazy.

Darci, coming in with a few last things from the old cabin, let out a yell. "Ginger!" All the girls stopped their work at the unexpected sharpness in her voice.

"Please sweep a little more gently." Darci forced a calm tone. "We don't want to sleep in dust piles tonight."

All the mattresses had been placed in the larger room at the back, which was to serve as sleeping quarters. Helen's bed, now next to Ginger's, faced the door leading to the front room. As she cleaned the window directly behind her bed, Helen could turn and see Ginger standing in the middle of the empty room, broom in hand.

Helen held her breath, wondering what Ginger would do now. To her surprise the red-headed girl just sighed and began to sweep carefully. No more dust clouds rose.

Later, as the bus bounced down the hill to the horses, Marge,

Dawn, and Helen clung to the seat in front of them.

"I like this back seat. It's like being on a roller coaster." Dawn shifted backward in an effort to stay on the slick seat. But every bump slid her closer to the edge again.

"I wonder if we'll get to ride today." Helen strained to see the horses. They had stopped at the corral again, and once more everyone lined up as Cowgirl Julie greeted them with a cheerful "Howdy." A green pickup pulled up next to the corral. Helen could see that it was loaded with blankets and saddles.

After a few minutes of brushing the horses Julie whistled for attention. A number of blankets had been draped over the corral by Pete, who now took one and demonstrated how to position it on the horse's back.

"We have a policy around here," Julie began, "that the first person who gets a blanket on a horse is the one who gets to ride it."

Everyone ran for a blanket as he sighted the horse he wanted. Helen turned to where Dandy was standing. No one had blanketed the pretty black-and-brown horse. Helen tossed her blanket over his broad back and returned for the saddle.

"Would you like some help?" 11-year-old Pete asked, and Helen shyly nodded. She glanced toward the white horse Ginger had blanketed and was not surprised to see the red head shake impatiently at one of the other young helpers as the girl began to cinch up the horse by herself.

When the saddling lesson was over, the campers led the horses to the pasture area and mounted them one by one. As Ginger swung her leg over the white mare the girl ahead of her started her animal off at a slow walk. The horse, with a mind of its own, reared and tossed the surprised rider into a thick patch of grass nearby.

Turning her pixie nose up in the air as she watched the counselor help the girl back to her feet, Ginger spoke up loudly, "If you don't know how to ride you shouldn't——" but she never finished her sentence. As she kicked her own horse to go, the animal gave an unexpected jerk, and the saddle shifted to the right, tossing Ginger into another patch of grass.

"If you don't know how to ride, what?" Marge asked innocently as her horse walked by Ginger, who was struggling to her feet and gently rubbing the back of her shoulder where she had landed.

Helen accepted Pete's offered lift up and then gently kicked her horse's sides. She waited, but nothing happened. Kicking Dandy a little harder, she waited again. Her third kick was none too gentle, and the horse took two steps, then stopped. *Now what?* thought Helen, a bit embarrassed, as she sat waiting.

"Got problems?" Pete rode up on the gray-and-white mare Helen had brushed the day before.

"This horse won't go!"

Pete slapped Dandy's hindquarters, but still the animal wouldn't budge.

Most of the other campers had left. Only Ginger, who was tightening her saddle, and Dawn, who stood nervously apart from the horses, her hands clasped behind her back, remained.

Pete slapped the horse once more, and Dandy again took a step or two. But all the slaps and kicks they tried wouldn't make him budge again.

"He gets stubborn sometimes!" Pete apologized. He dismounted and helped Helen off Dandy. "Here, try this one. Maybe she'll act like a lady for you, since Lady is her name."

But Lady wouldn't act like one. After more prods, kicks, and slaps Helen found herself fighting back tears. Riding time was almost over, and she hadn't been anywhere yet.

Julie rode up on another brown mare and offered to exchange with Helen.

Silently mounting for the third time, Helen couldn't believe it when the brown mare began to walk. Mounting Dandy, Pete took off at a fast trot toward another would-be rider who had taken an unexpected tumble. "Why wouldn't Dandy do that for me?" Helen asked Julie in wide-eyed surprise.

"Dandy is Pete's favorite. Dandy is also stubborn!"

Julie led the gray-and-white mare back to where Dawn stood watching the riders. Feeling suddenly very brave, Helen decided to see if she could make the brown mare trot. Kicking the horse's sides didn't work. Clicking her tongue at the horse didn't help either. Nothing seemed to work. "I guess I'm lucky you're even walking," Helen muttered to the mare, who meandered along as if she had all day to get nowhere.

Glancing over her shoulder, Helen caught a glimpse of Dawn shaking her head firmly as Julie held out her hands to help her on the gray mare. Dawn backed away a few steps and then motioned toward the little corral. As Helen turned forward in her saddle she couldn't help remembering how brave little Dawn was in the water. When she led her horse back to the corral later, Helen saw Dawn's short brown hair sticking up above the back of a small colt. Dawn gave her a big grin as she laid down the brush she had been using on the horse. "This one is more my size," she called cheerfully. "Maybe they'll let me ride this one tomorrow."

Marge rode up on a brown horse that stood tall and imposing next to Dawn's colt. She was smiling and looked very pleased with herself. Helen called out, "You know that horse you had last year? I think I found it."

Marge raised an eyebrow in question.

"After she walked a few minutes she put her head down, and I thought she was grazing. But the silly horse looked as if she were asleep."

"Did you get to ride at all?"

Helen frowned. "Not really. Maybe I'll get a better horse tomorrow. How about yours? He seems to be lively enough."

Marge beamed. "We did great. Went all the way around the pasture and then some before they called us in. How did you do, Dawn?"

Dawn glanced shyly at her friends. "I really would rather be swimming."

When the girls arrived at the pond they stripped off their jeans and

35

shirts and raced to the water.

"You forgot your shoes, Helen," Dawn called as she dived in.

"These are my extras. I can't swim and that stuff feels yucky under my feet."

Helen waded a bit in the shallow water and then attempted to swim. But the water flooded into her mouth and nose, and she came up sputtering. "Hey, Marge!" Helen called out later as she toweled off, "where's Ginger?"

"I don't know. You don't really think she drowned?" Alarm made Marge's voice sharp.

Helen shook her head. "I don't think she got off the bus."

Marge shrugged and swam to deeper water. "Maybe she went back to the cabin."

When the girls returned to the cabin, Ginger, Prissy, and the twins were already there.

"Isn't this neat?" The twins held up an object made of various sizes of balsa wood all nailed together to form interesting angles and points. It had been spray-painted. Susie's was a bright gold and Lucy's a light blue.

Prissy held hers up. It was a bright red.

On the floor between Helen and Ginger's bed lay a similar object, also in gold. Two pieces of wood had come off and lay nearby.

"What happened to this?" Helen retrieved the craft and examined it closely.

"Oh, Ginger decided to do crafts today instead of swim, but when she finished she didn't like it so she threw it on the floor!" The twins went back to admiring their own masterpieces. Using her shoe as a hammer, Helen tapped the two pieces back onto the form. She placed it on Ginger's bed and changed her clothes for line call.

When Ginger wandered back into the cabin nothing was said about the craft. The girl didn't know who had fixed it, but a strange feeling welled up inside Helen when she realized she had regretted missing crafts two days, while Ginger obviously wasn't enjoying doing hers.

At quiet time Helen took out her neglected book. A regular bookworm, she couldn't believe she hadn't read since Sunday. I'll finish it today for sure, she thought as she flopped onto her mattress. But she found herself glancing over at Ginger every few seconds. The redhead sat facing the door. Her face was half-turned from the rest of the girls, but her shoulders shook gently. Helen just knew that Ginger was crying.

Finally mustering up courage, Helen leaned toward Ginger. ''Is everything OK?''

''Why doesn't everyone just leave me alone?'' Ginger burst out as she jumped up and raced out the cabin door.

Darci and Tammy exchanged quick looks, and Tammy dashed after Ginger. In a few minutes the counselor returned alone and spoke quietly to Darci, who just shrugged and lay back down on her mattress.

After a long time, Ginger returned and without a word lay on her stomach on her own mattress and covered her head with her arms. Helen turned back to her book, but Ginger's tear-streaked face haunted every page.

At surprise time the youth director blew sharply on his whistle for attention. ''For our surprise today there will be canoeing for those who would like to, and afterward there will be free time and swimming for everyone!''

''Hooray!'' the campers yelled as boys and girls headed for the cabins to scramble back into wet swimsuits.

Helen settled into the nearest canoe as soon as they jumped off the bus and was surprised to find herself back to back with Ginger. Germie, one of the counselors, aided by Peaches, the bus driver, shoved the canoe out into the water. The two fellows took their positions and began to paddle smoothly to the center of the pond.

Helen glanced up in time to see Peaches wink at Germie. Suddenly the canoe began to rock mysteriously from side to side.

Ginger let out a frightened yell. Helen, guessing that the boys were playing games, just hung on tight.

Germie and Peaches, enjoying frightening at least one passenger, continued to paddle awhile and then began to rock the canoe again.

"Stop it! I want to get out. Stop it now!" Ginger yelled at the boys, who quit playing and paddled back to shore.

Peaches grinned at Helen. "I guess anybody who likes riding in the back seat of that bouncy old bus isn't too scared of a little canoe ride." With a wink he helped Germie haul the canoe back onto the beach. Most of the other girls and boys had decided that swimming and chasing one another was more fun than canoeing, and there were not enough people interested in the boats to go out again that day.

Feeling disappointed, Helen splashed in the water awhile, then sat on the beach watching the others.

Later, as the returning swimmers walked up the hill to the cabin, a strange sound off to one side caught their attention.

"What was that?" Marge squinted in the direction of the noise.

As the girls continued up the path the sound grew nearer.

"Isn't that some kind of cow?" Dawn pointed to a large dark object among the low trees and shrubs in back of the cabins. Suddenly, with a loud crash the animal charged through the brush.

"Help!" The girls let out a yell and raced toward their cabin.

Slamming the door behind them, they watched through the window as a large bull wandered about crashing through the trees and charging now and then at small birds that fluttered nearby.

A loud whistle pierced the air, and Helen could see bright shirts and pants as several of the counselors ran up the path and through the brush toward the bull, waving their hands and attempting to steer him back down the hill toward the pasture.

"How in the world did he get way up here?" Prissy's blue eyes grew bigger and bigger as she watched the bull and its pursuers retreat from view.

"That thing could have trampled us." Ginger's voice grew hysterical. "This place is dangerous. Snakes and bulls and canoes that tip over. I'm going home!" Silence filled the cabin as Ginger measured the reaction of the girls.

The counselors had gone to chase the bull. Left alone, the girls didn't have any words to encourage Ginger to stay.

Helen sat on her mattress staring at her shoes in silence.

"I am!" Ginger repeated loudly. "And no one can make me stay." Without a glance back she ran out the door and down the path.

Prissy and the twins stared at Dawn and Marge. Helen continued to stare at the floor. No one said a word.

4
More Surprises

As Helen changed her clothes for dinner she could hear the twins telling Prissy all their reasons for hoping Ginger wouldn't come back.

Helen glanced toward the counselors in the big room. I wonder whether they know how unwelcome Ginger has become, she thought.

"Girls, come here a minute, please." Darci's voice interrupted the unhappy thoughts and murmurings. "Please have a seat. I'd like to read you something." Opening her Bible, Darci began to read: "Whatsoever ye would that men should do to you, do ye even so to them." She eyed the frowning faces before her. "Let's have a word of prayer." The counselor paused as the girls slowly bowed their heads. "Dear Father in heaven, help us to remember that we are all Your children and we should treat one another as You would want us to."

Everyone was quiet for a moment, then Darci smiled. "That was as much directed at me as at you. I know none of us have been too happy with the way one of our cabin mates has been acting since she arrived, but none of us is perfect. Whether Ginger goes"—Darci paused and stared levelly at the girls—"or whether she stays, we are to remember to act nicer to one another the rest of this week." Darci turned to the door, then stopped and looked back at the girls. "Our *cabin* may have passed inspection every day this week, but what about our *hearts?*"

In silence the girls filed out onto the path for village line call. Without a word they followed the counselors to the cook's garage and lined up for supper.

Helen's spirits lifted when she saw the serving pan heaped with steaming macaroni and cheese. With a big grin she asked for a large helping. "That's my favorite food," she informed the woman who served her. In the cafeteria Helen found a seat at one of the tables. She said a short prayer of thanks and eagerly dished up a forkful of the treat. But her spirits crashed again with the first bite. Waiting a minute, she tried again. But the second bite was no different. "How can they ruin macaroni and cheese?" Helen turned the plate around and carefully tried the beans and salad. "Well, they're OK anyway." After finishing off the rest of her supper she eyed her "favorite food" once more. Mom's always tasted so great. "I can't believe anybody can make it taste as bad as I think that did. I'll try one more time," Helen resolved aloud to no one in particular. But the next few bites tasted no better. Reluctantly, and with a definite feeling that something was missing, she dumped the remainder of her plate into the trash.

"If this keeps up," Helen informed Marge as they headed for the camp store, "my stomach is going to think my throat is cut."

Marge grinned back. "I thought the macaroni and cheese was delicious. You've got to be the pickiest eater I've ever met." Marge patted her own rounded waistline. "My Mom wishes I were a little pickier sometimes. I can't help it. I *like* food."

Helen stopped in her tracks. "You sound like my mother. She always says I'm too fussy about my food."

Returning to the cabin later for her flashlight, Helen was only mildly surprised to see Ginger's suitcase still at the foot of her bed.

"I don't think she's going to leave," Helen told Marge as they walked toward campfire.

The music didn't brighten the evening for Helen tonight. She found herself staring into the flames only vaguely aware of what song was being sung.

Raising her eyes as Pastor Jack began to talk, Helen spotted Mrs. Layton directly across the campfire from her. Next to her sat Ginger.

Helen dropped her eyes to the campfire again. "I wonder if that's where she's been all afternoon, talking to the girls' director." Helen hardly heard a word of Pastor Jack's talk.

"Hey!" Marge punched her in the ribs. "I said it's time to go."

Helen jumped up. Campfire was over. Lagging behind her unit, she felt as if a heavy weight lay on her 10-year-old shoulders.

In silence she undressed and put on her pajamas. Crawling between the sheets, she lay staring into the dark.

Ginger's suitcase lay untouched where it had been earlier. No Ginger lay on the mattress next to hers. Helen continued to stare into the dark.

Sometime later Helen was wakened by the sound of a suitcase opening, and movement close by caused her to catch her breath. The suitcase closed again. A few minutes later someone lay down on the mattress.

"Ginger is not leaving." Helen formed the words in her mind. "Ginger is not leaving." A tear slid down her cheek and dampened the pillow.

* * *

"Are you feeling OK?" Marge's face showed concern as Unit One lined up for general line call. "You've hardly spoken since you got up this morning."

Helen just nodded. Mechanically she mouthed the words to the pledges and woodenly followed her unit to the breakfast line.

The hot pancakes helped fill her empty stomach, but she ate them slowly, hardly tasting their fluffy sweetness.

Even the bouncy ride to the horse corral didn't lift her spirits.

She brushed and blanketed a white mare, touching the horse's nose and speaking softly while she waited for Pete to finish saddling the horse. "You're going to be good and walk for me, aren't you? You're not going to be stubborn like those others."

42

Pete turned a broad smile on Helen. "You like horses, don't you?"

Helen nodded and continued to pat the horse. "Yes. We used to graze horses for a man when we lived out in the country. Sometimes he would saddle one up and let us ride. But it was such a big horse I couldn't get on by myself."

"Do you think you can get on this one?" Pete stepped back and held the horse steady. "Go ahead and try." His smile made Helen blush.

Placing her left foot in the stirrup, Helen tried to reach the saddle horn and the back of the saddle to help lift herself up. After two tries she was halfway on. Pete reached over, and giving a small shove helped her the rest of the way. "Almost." Helen breathed heavily a moment, and her cheeks were bright red.

"You'll get it yet!"

A smile tugged at her lips as Pete helped lead the horse to the pasture gate. Giving the mare a sharp whack and yelling, "Go, girl!" Pete stepped aside.

The horse took a few steps, and Helen found herself smiling hopefully. But the grin soon faded when the mare stopped and no amount of prodding would make her go again.

"Sorry, Helen, they just don't seem to want to go." Pete helped her down.

Ginger, on the brown-and-black beauty, passed Helen as she stood by the fence. "I don't know why *you're* having so much trouble. These horses walk just fine."

Pete flashed Ginger a frown as her horse trotted by.

"Let's try this one over here." Pete unsaddled the mare and saddled a dark-brown horse that was tied nearby. But Helen had no better success this time. The horse would walk a few steps, then stand still, walk a few steps, then stop again.

Just then Julie called Pete to help her do something, so Helen was left alone to try to make the horse walk.

Before she had gone more than a few yards the bus honked, and

Peaches whistled loudly for the campers. It was time to go swimming. A very discouraged Helen climbed aboard the bus. Instead of taking the back seat with Dawn and Marge, she sat next to a window about halfway up the bus. She barely saw the scenery as they bounced along the road. Fighting back tears she bit her lip in an effort not to cry.

Helen didn't remove her jeans and shirt, but sat on the beach area at the swimming hole watching the others splash. "Look at the way Dawn swims, and she's only 8." Helen wrapped her arms around her legs and rested her chin on her knees.

Back at the cabin, the other girls quickly changed for lunch, cheerfully pulling off soaked jeans and wet swimsuits. Their cheerfulness did not reach Helen through her dark cloud. The day became even gloomier when she spied a piece of driftwood in the trash. On it was fastened a tiny fake bird and bits of flowers. She started to lift it from the trash, but drew back her hand.

At lunch Helen sat slightly apart from her unit. She wondered where Ginger was, and was surprised to see her sitting with the unit instead of at the opposite row of tables. Although Ginger wasn't talking with anyone, she was eating her lunch for a change. Come to think of it, Helen thought, nobody had to remake her bed or put her flashlight and Bible in the proper place this morning. She's been awfully quiet for Ginger. Then she remembered Ginger's remark about the horses at the corral. No, she's still Ginger.

Helen didn't bother to go to the camp store after eating, but returned immediately to the cabin, where she stretched out on her mattress with her hands behind her head and stared at the ceiling.

In a few minutes the other girls crowded into the room to lie on their mattresses for quiet time, but Helen continued to stare at the ceiling in silence. It wasn't long before her decision became firm. Jumping to her feet, she crossed to the big room where the counselors lay resting.

Darci glanced up from the book she was reading. "Everything OK, kid?" A worried look crossed her usually cheerful face.

"May I go see Mrs. Layton? I'd like to—to talk to her."

Darci nodded her assent, and Helen quickly covered the distance to the door and almost flew down the path. "Mrs. Layton will understand. She's nice to talk to. She'll let me go." Helen felt small pebbles beneath her tennis shoes as she passed the last of the girls' cabins. She'd never been this far before except with her unit or in the bus, but she knew where to find the counselors' cabins. "I hope she's alone." Helen slowed up. "She's got to let me go home. She just has to." There were no tears now. Only a firm, almost angry, resolve. "If Ginger won't go, then I will!"

Doryne Layton sat on the edge of her bunk writing letters when the serious-faced girl entered. Smiling brightly, she motioned for Helen to have a seat next to her. "How are you? Are you enjoying camp? I've hardly seen you this week. You're getting a nice tan. Must be doing a lot of swimming."

45

"I don't know how to swim, and they're not teaching us how like I thought they would. We just go out there and splash around, unless you already know how to swim. And the bottom is too yucky to wade."

Doryne's smile faded slightly. "I know," she said slowly. "They're going to fill in the bottom with sand and gravel. They had hoped to have a lot of classes this week, but things didn't work out quite as they planned this time. You know, this is the first camp ever at NVR. They're still getting organized."

Helen ignored Mrs. Layton's attempts to cheer her. "I haven't had crafts once, and it was on my list. The horses won't walk, and that's what I wanted to do most." Tears threatened to spill over. "And Ginger's impossible," she blurted out suddenly.

Doryne's smile faded completely. Laying her writing tablet aside, she picked up a small handkerchief that lay neatly folded nearby and offered it to Helen.

"I thought she was going to go home." Helen dabbed at her eyes with the handkerchief. "But she didn't."

"Would that have made camp nicer for you—if Ginger *had* gone home?" Doryne's voice was gentle and kind.

Helen stared at the handkerchief in her hand. "I don't know. But her being here isn't making it any better."

"What if I told you something about Ginger, something that might help you understand her better?"

Helen blinked at the youthful counselor. Nothing will make me understand her better, she thought angrily. She's just being ugly and difficult, and everybody just puts up with her. But Helen said nothing as she absently twisted the handkerchief into a knot.

Doryne hesitated a moment, then reached out and touched Helen's shoulder. "You're a very fortunate girl to have a mother and a father and a sister and brothers who all love you very much." She paused a moment, wondering just what to say. Then she continued. "Ginger's father died when she was 4. She doesn't remember him at all. Her mother died two months ago of cancer. She has no brothers.

No sisters. Just before her mother died she told Ginger she'd be going to live with her mother's sister, Ann Rorke, an Adventist. Ginger's mother was not a Christian. I met Mrs. Rorke when she brought Ginger to camp. She warned me there might be problems.'' Doryne collected her thoughts a moment before continuing. ''Ginger's mother and Mrs. Rorke were very close until Ann joined the church when Ginger was about 5. All these years Ginger didn't even really know she had an aunt until suddenly she had to go and live with her. Mrs. Rorke hoped that sending her to camp might help her to feel more comfortable with Adventist girls her age before she starts church school this fall.''

Helen had slowly unknotted the handkerchief and now sat staring at the attractive counselor. But she saw only the faces of her own mother and father as she tried to picture what it would be like to lose *both* of them. And to have no sister and no brothers either! Helen shivered slightly and then glanced down at her hands.

''Oh, I've messed up your hanky.'' She smoothed out the wrinkles as best she could and passed the handkerchief back to the counselor. ''And thank you.'' Helen's eyes were bright now, and she wondered whether Mrs. Layton realized she meant more than just a Thank you for the handkerchief. ''Thank you for *everything.*''

Doryne touched the younger girl's cheek. ''You're very welcome.''

Deep in thought, Helen walked slowly back to the cabin. With a start, she halted on the path. ''I forgot to tell her I wanted to go home!'' she chuckled softly as she continued on her way. ''Well, there's no rush. Might as well give camp another try.''

She was surprised to find the cabin empty. Glancing at her watch, she realized everyone was out for the ''surprise.''

Helen grinned. ''I wouldn't mind missing it if it is another camp development session.''

As she started back down the path she met Tammy coming up the road. ''Hello there! Everyone is on a nature walk. I came back for my binoculars. Wait up and I'll show you where our unit is.''

Helen hummed softly to herself as she walked down the path with the counselor.

"I'm glad to see you're in better spirits now."

Helen glanced up at the older girl. She hadn't realized her feelings had shown. "Much better now, thank you."

At campfire that evening Debbie, the guitarist, did not strike a chord and ask for favorites as usual, but held up two fingers for silence instead. "Quiet, you guys. We've got something different for you tonight."

As a hush settled over the circle of campers, Debbie continued. "All those songs some of you've been practicing for the talent show will now be sung before a live audience." Debbie placed a hand over her eyes, shielding them as she stared out at the boys and girls. "You are alive out there, aren't you?"

Laughter broke out, and Debbie clapped. "Good. Now on with the talent show."

Helen enjoyed the music and giggled at the efforts of her fellow campers to be real professionals.

At the very end of the talent show one of the girl counselors sang "Jesus Is the Sweetest Name I Know."

A hush fell over the group. Helen glanced at Ginger, who stared quietly at the singer.

As Pastor Jack spoke, Helen noticed that Ginger did not fidget as usual. She didn't break small twigs or draw pictures in the dirt with sticks. Instead, she sat quietly, drinking in all that Pastor Jack said about Jesus and His love for everyone and how much He wants us all to be happy.

"Satan is the one that causes all the unpleasant things to happen, because he wants us to blame Jesus. If we think Jesus is the one trying to make us miserable we won't want to love Him, right? And Satan will have won. Jesus is just waiting until we all see Satan for what he really is. And then it will all be over. Jesus will destroy Satan, and unhappiness with him. Realizing how much Jesus loves us is a lot easier when we remember He even let Satan try to make Him sin and even get Him nailed to the cross. But it turned out all right in the end. It's not what happens to a person, but how he accepts it, that really makes the difference.''

As everyone bowed his head for prayer Ginger bowed her head too. Helen smiled softly as she closed her eyes. All the way back to the cabin she hummed to herself:

"Jesus is the sweetest name I know,
   And He's just the same as His lovely name,
   And that's the reason why I love Him so;
   Oh, Jesus is the sweetest name I know."

As the girls entered the cabin, Darci reached for the electric switch. To everyone's delight the room was flooded with light, and a cheer went up. ''They told me the electricity would be in tonight, but I hardly believed it.''

''No more dressing in the dark.'' Marge flicked off her flashlight and switched on the light in the back room, where the girls slept.

''No more stumbling to the bathroom in the dark.'' Dawn checked the light in each of the bathrooms. They both flicked on with welcome brightness.

The girls cheered until the counselors had to call a halt, then they pulled their pajamas out of the suitcases and began to change. Prissy giggled as she held up her shorty pajamas. ''They're wrong side out. I would have put them on that way.''

One by one the girls put their clothes away and tumbled onto their mattresses. Reluctantly, they watched as Darci flicked off the lights and the familiar darkness settled in again.

Helen lay in bed humming, a soft smile playing around her lips. But the tune died on her lips as she began to sniff the air. A strange odor drifted in from the window over her bed and quickly filled the room.

''Phew!'' Marge pulled the sheet over her head. Dawn and Prissy soon followed her example.

''What is it?'' asked the twins, coughing and holding their noses.

''A skunk,'' Ginger announced simply as she buried her head in her pillow and pulled it around her face.

Helen was pleased at the lack of sarcasm in Ginger's voice. But she wasn't too happy about the odor.

"We could close the windows, but it is way too hot!" commented Tammy.

"Great choice." Darci laughed as she, too, held her nose. "Die from the heat or from that terrible odor."

"Maybe the skunk will leave," Helen called out hopefully.

"Even if it does that odor won't," Tammy called back.

But eventually, and in spite of the smell, the girls quieted down. Outside, a small black-and-white creature, tired of its current location, slowly wandered away unaware of the smelly reminder it had left behind.

5

Improvements

Helen did not open her eyes at once, but lay in bed enjoying the early-morning quiet. With a deep sigh she turned on her back and listened to the soft voices around her. Marge and Dawn are awake, she thought with a smile, as their voices drifted to her. The twins aren't yet. With their almost constant giggling it was easy to tell when Lucy and Susie woke up and when they fell asleep.

Suddenly Helen remembered, and her eyes flew open. Wrinkling her freckled nose, she sniffed the air, then stretched out with a satisfied yawn. That awful smell was almost gone.

"Up and at it!" Tammy's cheerful voice interrupted the peaceful quiet.

"Ugh." Frowning slightly, Helen dragged herself reluctantly from her mattress bed. Across from her, Ginger sat cross-legged, rubbing the sleep from her eyes. "Good morning. Isn't it a great day?" Helen said pleasantly.

Ginger stopped rubbing at her eyes and stared with her mouth half open. Helen smiled again and turned back to making her bed.

When Ginger finished making up her own bed a small section near Helen's side remained untucked. Helen reached across the mattress and quickly tucked it in with another friendly smile. Ginger mumbled thanks and dropped her flashlight onto the pillow.

Darci called the girls together for morning worship. "Let's open our Bibles to Matthew 6 this morning, please."

There was silence except for the faint ruffling of the pages.

"I'd like us to read together the Lord's Prayer."

" 'Our Father, which art in heaven, hallowed be thy name.' " Helen glanced at Ginger, whose long red hair shielded her face from view.

" 'Thy kingdom come. Thy will be done—' " Helen continued to study her cabin mates and counselors as she recited the verses from memory.

" '—in earth, as it is in heaven. Give us this day our daily bread.' " It really isn't so bad here after all, she thought, flushing as she realized how close she had come to leaving. Her thoughts returned to the words of Jesus' prayer.

" 'And forgive us our debts, as we forgive our debtors.' "

Helen glanced at Ginger again. The girl was staring straight ahead, her lips not moving. A tiny tear slid down her cheek.

Thank You for helping me to forgive Ginger, Lord, and please forgive me for not trying to be friendlier to her.

" 'And lead us not into temptation, but deliver us from evil: For thine is the kingdom, and the power, and the glory, for ever. Amen.' "

As the girls knelt for prayer Darci requested that they hold hands in a circle.

Helen smiled shyly at Ginger as she held her left hand out to her. Ginger hesitated a moment, but finally reached over and allowed her hand to lay loosely in Helen's.

"Dear Father in heaven," Darci prayed softly as a reverent quiet filled the cabin, "thank You for Your loving care through the night and for this new day. May it be filled with joys, as well as adventures. Help us to love one another as You have loved us. In Jesus' name we ask, thanking You for hearing our prayer. Amen."

No one moved for a few seconds, as if to hold on to something special as long as possible. Suddenly Ginger withdrew her hands from Darci's and Helen's, and the moment was over.

"General line call!" Tammy called out, and the girls hurried to put away their Bibles and be the first cabin to line up.

It wasn't hard for Helen to get next to Ginger in line call and to fall in behind her in the breakfast line. "Would you like to sit with me at breakfast, Ginger?" she asked quickly as they picked up their trays.

Ginger shrugged silently. Helen followed the redhead to the cafeteria and placed her tray next to Marge's, then patted the next seat. "Sit here, Ginger." Ginger glanced at Marge, who looked quickly at Helen, then back at her food.

Without a word, Ginger carried her tray to the other side of the big table and took a seat apart from her cabin mates.

Marge chewed hard on her pancakes, then turned suddenly to Helen. "Why did you do that after all the mean things she's done?"

"I was just forgiving her her debts."

Marge blushed, then returned to her pancakes. But she ate more slowly, stopping ever so often to glance at Ginger.

After returning to the cabin for her towel and the camera she had so carefully tucked away and completely forgotten about during the first few days of camp, Helen hurried to the square. Boarding the bus, she paused a moment for Ginger, but the other girl pushed past and crowded into a seat where two girls from another cabin were sitting. Feeling let down, Helen moved on to the back and joined Dawn and Marge.

"You're really going out of your way to be nice to her today, aren't you?"

"Sometimes people aren't what they seem. They may be nice underneath if you give them a chance."

Marge shook her head, and the three of them rode the rest of the way in silence. Once Dawn opened her mouth to speak, but closed it again as she caught Marge's quick glance.

Helen waited until Marge and Dawn were off the bus before she climbed down the steps. Taking care not to bang her camera on the corral rails, she climbed to her favorite perch. Julie and Pete were nowhere in sight. The campers walked about restlessly and murmured loudly as they waited.

A noise from the big pasture caught everyone's attention. The children turned in time to see some of the workers chasing cows and horses down the dirt path.

"Let's go watch 'em," yelled one of the boys. Everyone raced to the fence and scrambled for a better view.

"What's going on?" Helen called out to Pete when he stopped running long enough to mop his forehead.

"Aw, most of the cows and horses got out somehow, and we're trying to round them up." Irritation edged his voice. He dropped his hat back into place and let out a frustrated yell as he raced after a stray cow that teasingly went up to the open gate, then dodged playfully away.

The boys and girls laughed at the sight of the workers trying to herd the stubborn animals back into the pasture area. A few of the campers yelled out directions and whooped as the cows and horses dashed here and there.

Helen snatched up her camera and tried to snap a few shots. Everything moved so fast she soon stopped trying to catch them on the run. Finally she snapped one of Pete as he threw his hat after the stubborn cow he had been herding in vain.

"You need a movie camera for this," a voice chuckled next to Helen, who almost fell off the fence as she glanced down to see Ginger laughing as hard as everyone else and mopping her eyes. "Isn't that a sight?" She pointed to one of the workers trying to ride the black-and-brown beauty bareback.

Helen smiled at the sound of Ginger's musical laughter. "Do you have a movie camera?"

Ginger shook her head. "I wanted a camera like that one," she said, pointing to Helen's, "but I never got it." She stopped laughing and stared solemnly at the workers for a moment.

I shouldn't have asked that, Helen thought with a sigh and quickly set about trying to make things right. "I got this one by selling cards and things. I didn't think it would get here in time for camp, but it came to the house the Friday before we left. I prayed a lot for that camera. It's really neat and so little."

Ginger studied Helen thoughtfully. "You don't *really* believe in prayer, do you?"

Helen stared back. "Sure. I've prayed about a lot of things. One time I wanted a hamster real bad, but we couldn't afford to buy one. About a year after I started praying for it I got one, free, from a friend of ours. Cage and everything."

Ginger sniffed. "A year later. That sounds as though God wasn't too concerned."

"Sometimes God says Wait. Or maybe He just wanted to see if I really and truly wanted one. Anyway, I have one now. And God sent it to me. And I got my camera in time for camp. God didn't wait a year that time," Helen said with a grin.

"God doesn't answer my prayers." Ginger's voice was cold and hard. "I prayed for almost a year that my mother wouldn't die. He let her die anyway. That's some answer." Without another word she turned and walked off.

Helen stared at the little camera in her hand. She wondered what she would have said if Ginger had waited for her to answer.

Sitting by the twins at lunchtime, Helen wondered how anybody could giggle and eat at the same time, but Lucy and Susie managed. Sometimes she would start to laugh at how silly they seemed, but then she'd almost choke on her food. "You two are something," she finally managed to say as they cleared away their plates and trays. The twins glanced at each other and giggled again.

Helen snapped a picture or two of the boys and girls in the cafeteria, then dangled the camera by its strap from her arm while she browsed in the camp store. When she returned to the cabin she placed the camera on the windowsill, where it would be handy, then stretched out for quiet time.

Tammy's "Rise and shine!" interrupted Helen's dreams. She stretched lazily and turned on one side.

Marge, attempting to drag Dawn out of bed, lost her grip and bumped into the side wall. A slight tremor shook the cabin. "You're going to knock the cabin down, and we'll have to move back up the hill." Helen giggled at Marge's wry face.

"That's a terrible thought," Marge panted as she continued to pull a reluctant Dawn to her feet.

"Surprise time!" Darci called out as the counselors grabbed their binoculars and Darci's bird book.

"It's a nature walk." Dawn suddenly brightened up and raced after the counselors. Behind, she left a flustered Marge, hands on hips.

Prissy grabbed her tennis shoes and almost tripped over Helen as she raced for the door.

"Oh, I'm glad it's a walk. Maybe I can take a picture of those dinosaur tracks they were telling us about," Helen said to Marge, who was pulling on her jeans.

"How about getting a picture of that huge snail shell you found the other day?" Marge reminded. "Hey, what are you looking for?"

56

"That's funny." Helen frowned as she stood staring at the empty windowsill. "I know I left my camera right here somewhere."

"Let's go," Tammy called out impatiently as she dashed back into the cabin for a notebook and pencil. The girls smoothed their beds with one hand, grabbed their shoes with the other, and hobbled down the hill trying to put on first one shoe then the other while they ran.

"You know what I think?" Marge panted as they lined up in the square.

"No, what?" Helen hastily tied her last sneaker.

"Ginger took it."

Helen stood up quickly and glared at Marge. "Why would you say a thing like that?"

"I heard her saying she wanted one like it down at the horse corral this morning."

"And she didn't go to sleep at quiet time," Dawn added in a soft whisper. "She was reading when I dozed off."

"She was reading when we woke up, too," Marge added quickly, as if that settled the issue.

"She didn't take it. You aren't being fair!" Helen couldn't believe her ears.

"All right then." Marge drew herself up tall. "If she didn't take it, *where is it?*"

Helen opened her mouth, then closed it again. Ginger *didn't* take it, she wanted to protest. But Marge and Dawn were determined about one thing. Until they knew where the camera was, Ginger was guilty in their eyes.

Helen searched through her suitcase and all around the mattress during the break after supper, hoping desperately she would find the camera and clear Ginger. But all her searching only turned up one stray comb belonging to Prissy. Tossing the comb onto the younger girl's bed, Helen sank down onto her own mattress with a heavy sigh. For a second her eyes lingered on Ginger's closed suitcase.

"What if——?" but she shook her head sharply. "She didn't!

57

She *wouldn't!''* Dropping her head into her hands, she sighed heavily. ''It has to turn up. *It just has to.''*

Later, at campfire, Helen found herself staring at Ginger. The question still haunted her. *Did she?* Shaking her head to clear her mind, she made herself listen to Pastor Jack.

''It's not easy being different,'' the young pastor spoke seriously. ''A lot of young people about your age begin to feel that the Adventist rules and way of living are too hard because it makes them seem strange to their non-Adventist friends. But God has given us all our health rules and moral rules for a reason—to protect us, just as your parents give you rules to protect you.'' He paused and grinned. ''When you were little your mom warned you not to play in the street or touch the hot stove or climb on rickety cabinets—and you probably wanted to anyway. She knew you could get hurt even before you understood that. Well, God's rules are kind of like that. We may not understand them now. Maybe your friends will make fun of you, and people might even call you strange. But God's rules have reasons, and someday you'll understand them.''

Once more Helen shifted her glance to Ginger and was surprised to find the girl listening intently to the pastor.

''The important thing is to know why we are different and to have the right attitude about it. If you're different because your parents or teachers or someone else is trying to make you do things the way that person wants things done, whether you want to do it that way or not, then you'll be miserable. And instead of people thinking, Hey, that guy or that girl has something good I want, they'll be turned off by the grumps and say that religion isn't for them. But we shouldn't act as if we're better than everybody else, either, just because we follow God's rules. That's what happened to the Jews.''

Helen found herself listening so carefully to Pastor Jack that she forgot all about Ginger and the mysterious disappearance of her camera.

''If we accept God's rules because we know Jesus loves us—really loves and wants only what is best for us—then we'll be happy to do or not do what He says we should or should not do. And we'll do so cheerfully. Then our friends will say, Hey, that kid has got something and I want to know what it is. A grumpy Christian isn't really a Christian at all, because *Christian* means being like Christ, and Christ never had a case of the grumps.''

The campers couldn't resist smiling as Pastor Jack paused a moment. But then he continued in a soft voice, ''If you've been afraid to do things God's way because you didn't want to be strange, or if you've been following God's rules only because you felt you had to, I want you to bow your head and pray that God will help you to love Jesus so much you'll *want* to follow His way every day—because He loves you!''

Several heads bowed in the darkness around the campfire. Then Pastor Jack closed his eyes and prayed.

After the closing song, Helen flipped the switch on her flashlight, then groaned as the light refused to come on. ''The battery must be dead,'' she muttered. Since the other campers were already beginning to leave, she hurried to catch up with them. At least I can walk in their light back to the cabin, she thought hopefully.

As she picked her way over the rocky ground as carefully as she could in the dark, Helen's ankle suddenly gave way, and she hit the hard ground. Limping to a rock, she rubbed her throbbing foot and tried to ignore the pain long enough to rejoin the quickly disappearing group.

As a few stragglers came up behind her, Helen called out, ''Can I walk with you? My flashlight is out.''

Ginger's voice answered back, ''What happened to your foot?''

''I twisted my ankle. It's not too bad, but I just can't run very well.''

Ginger slowed up for Helen, who tried to limp along as quickly as possible.

Ginger did not speak as they walked along together. ''What did you think of campfire tonight?'' Helen asked suddenly, trying to break the silence.

"How can anyone enjoy being as odd as Adventists are?" A faint hint of sarcasm edged Ginger's voice.

"I don't think we really think of ourselves as odd. We're just Bible believers, my Mom always says."

"All that about following the rules because you love Jesus and He loves you. How can you love a God who lets people get sick and die when somebody needs them?" Ginger stopped suddenly and faced Helen fiercely. "What would you think of God if He let both your father and your mother die and left you to live with a woman who believes in a strange religion?"

Helen didn't answer for a moment. She felt uneasy again. Ginger had such hard questions. Before she could speak Ginger began walking, striding ahead.

Helen suddenly found her voice. "Mrs. Layton said God doesn't make people sick. Satan does. And Pastor Jack said we'll understand it all in heaven."

Ginger stopped again. Anger was rising in her voice. "I want to understand *now!*"

Helen drew herself up tall as she faced Ginger. Her mind formed a silent prayer: Dear God, help me say the right things. "The Bible says that God knows what is best for us. Maybe—maybe your mother's dying was better than hurting all the time. Maybe living with your aunt will help you to do something God wants you to do. Something special. I don't know, but Mamma said God knows everything and that He loves us. When your mother and father died, Jesus cried too. He doesn't want anyone to die. But if you love Him, *really* love Him with all your heart, and if they loved Him too, then when Jesus comes back you'll see them again. And you'll never be sad or sick or anything again. Right now you just have to trust Him, Ginger. You just have to trust Him."

Ginger began walking slowly up the trail once more. All the other campers had disappeared over the hill ahead, and her flashlight made a lonely little path of light. Helen limped along behind as quickly as she could.

"I miss them so much." Tears choked Ginger's words.

"Jesus knows that. He'll help you—if you want Him to." Helen stopped walking, and Ginger stopped too. "Ginger, do you really think we're so strange?"

The girl's mouth opened to answer, then snapped shut again. Turning, she began to walk away quickly. Helen found herself having to run painfully to keep up.

6

Preparations

We have something a little different this morning," Darci announced after the girls had finished their morning group worship time and closed their Bibles. "Tomorrow is Sabbath, and we'll be having Sabbath school in the cafeteria and worship hour at the camp-council clearing, up the hill. So"—she paused and grinned mischievously—"that means we'll need chairs up there. *Lots* of chairs. They're expecting *hoards* of visitors."

A chorus of groans went up as the girls pictured themselves struggling up that rocky path with folding chairs tucked under their arms.

"Helen," Darci said as she turned to the still-limping camper, "because of your ankle you may stay at the cafeteria and help set up chairs there."

Helen smiled. "Thanks!" The thought of hobbling up that hill lugging chairs had not been too pleasant.

As the girls marched down the path to general line call Marge poked Helen in the back. "Look over there." A large tent had been pitched in the clearing. Already the boys were hard at work setting up long rows of tables and unloading chairs from a pickup that stood nearby.

"That's where we're eating today so they can get things ready for Sabbath school in the cafeteria," Darci announced as they lined up. General line call and breakfast flew by, and the campers hurried to finish Friday preparations. Excitement at the prospect of seeing family and friends the next day filled everybody with extra energy. Helen almost managed to forget her ankle as she quickly set up one chair after another, helping first in the big tent and then in the cafeteria.

Riding in the bus later, everyone tried to talk at once. ''Mom said she's going to bring all the relatives tomorrow to spend the day,'' the twins giggled and chirped as they bounced up and down. Their blonde hair bobbed, and their freckles fairly danced. At 8 years of age, they had never been away from home this long before. ''I want to tell them about the skunk,'' Lucy burst out.

''And I'm going to tell them about the snake,'' Susie chimed in.

''I'm going to tell Mom I can get up on a horse all by myself,'' Prissy fairly beamed. ''And I can make my own bed and—and all sorts of things.''

Helen smiled at Prissy's excitement. She marveled at all that Prissy, an only child who could hardly tie her own shoes when she first arrived, had accomplished in just one week.

''Your mom won't even recognize you,'' Helen laughed. Prissy no longer seemed shy and scared as she laughed and talked with the other campers.

''I'd just as soon my folks didn't bring any visitors,'' Marge called over the din. ''They wouldn't believe this crazy bunch I've been rooming with.''

Helen reached across Dawn to punch Marge in the ribs just as the bus jerked to a halt at the corral, and the three girls fell on the floor in front of the back seat in a jumbled heap of arms and legs.

''They ought to engrave our names on this seat,'' Dawn giggled as she struggled up from the pile of girls. ''I almost feel it belongs to us.''

''The Three Camping Nuts were here,'' Helen sang out as they all tumbled off the bus in a fresh burst of laughter.

Helen was limping less now. She climbed the fence to the second railing with ease and tried to locate the spotted mare she had ridden the day before. "Maybe today we'll make it all the way around—twice even," she said as she eagerly saddled and mounted the mare without assistance. Then she grinned at Marge, who was saddling a solid-black horse. Helen picked up the reins and moved easily away. "I'm beginning to feel like a regular horseman, after all," she called back.

"More like a horsegirl if you ask me." Marge glanced up over her glasses at Helen.

Helen grinned and flicked the reins to the mare's side. "I'm sure glad Marge is talking to me again," she told her horse. Helen fondly remembered Marge's concern at the time of the accident. The chubby girl had done everything she could to be helpful during the hours that Helen's ankle was so sore.

As Marge pulled her horse up next to Helen's they smiled at each other and rode along quietly for a while.

"Isn't that a beautiful sight?" Helen pointed to the hills off beyond the ranch. A herd of white and black cattle grazed near a small brick house. The sky seemed extra bright and clear. "Sure wish I had a picture of that."

For a moment an uneasy silence settled over the two girls as each remembered the unpleasantness surrounding the disappearance of Helen's camera.

"I'm sorry about the way I acted yesterday," Marge ventured at last.

"That's OK," Helen returned quickly, then kicked the sides of her horse and called over her shoulder, "Last one to the big oak tree is a rotten egg."

Not to be outdone, Marge urged her own mount into a trot and followed close behind.

The two girls finished circling the pasture just as the bus pulled up and Peaches, leaning out the window, yelled, "All aboard or else you walk." His toothy grin flashed in the bright sun.

"That water ought to feel good today," Marge panted as she dismounted and started for the bus, wiping the beads of perspiration

64

from her forehead.

"Helen!"

Helen stopped short and turned to see Pete running from the little corral toward her. His face seemed red under his tan, and he stammered slightly. "Today's the last day of riding and stuff." Pete's blush grew more obvious as he glanced nervously away from Helen and toward the bus. "But I just wanted to—well, to see if you think you might be back next year."

"I hope so. I like this camp." Helen grinned sheepishly at the young man.

"I'm not much for writing and stuff like that." Pete kicked a solid-looking rock for a few moments. "But—well, if you ever have a minute and want to drop a line—I live here." He jerked a thumb over his shoulder toward the mobile homes. "And, well, you could write and tell me if you've been doing any more horseback riding."

"Helen!" Marge and Dawn chorused from the bus.

"Thanks for everything, Pete. Maybe I'll write. Now I better go, or Peaches *will* make me walk."

"I'm sorry about your ankle. Hope it gets all better right quick."

Helen smiled at Pete in silence, then limped onto the bus. From her seat at the back she watched as his figure grew smaller in the distance.

"Looks like Miss Skinny here has a boyfriend." Marge's playful poke in her ribs passed without notice.

"Maybe I can talk my family into coming camping here sometime this summer," Helen said wistfully as she turned forward. But her mind was elsewhere as she half listened to all the giggles and chatter on the bus.

"How did your lesson go today, Dawn?" Helen asked the 8-year-old as they clambered off the bus at the water hole.

"I rode all the way around the corral," Dawn announced proudly. "Julie said if I had another week here I might manage to get out of the little corral and do some real riding." She sighed heavily.

"When you get home are you going to give up swimming and devote all your time to horses from now on?" Helen asked in mock seriousness.

"Never!" Dawn announced with a shiver. "I'd rather dive off the highest diving board in the world than get on one of those things if I don't have to!"

Helen shook her head in disbelief. She couldn't picture anybody being afraid of a horse.

"I'm dying of thirst." Helen rubbed her forehead and throat. The day seemed to become hotter by the second. The few sheltering clouds had evaporated, and the sun beat down unmercifully.

The swimming hole felt extra good, in spite of its still-mushy bottom. "I'm so thirsty I could almost drink this awful stuff." Helen stretched out in the shallow water and let the small waves from the boats and swimmers wash over her. Back at the cabin, she didn't wait to get her wet clothes off before heading to the water cooler.

She pushed the button on the spigot and watched as a small stream
66

of water trickled into her cup. Gulping it down, she pushed and pushed at the button, but no more water could be coaxed out.

"Here." Marge tipped the cooler forward, and Helen tried again. She managed to fill the cup almost to its top before the water gave out completely.

"There's a fountain by the cafeteria," Darci reminded the hot campers. "With all the extra work to do today I haven't had a chance to fill up the cooler."

Helen's appetite had waned to an all-time low. At dinner she drank the juice she received in the line, and then filled her cup at the water fountain. The ice-cold water sent sudden chills over her. "Oh, my teeth are cold now!" She filled her cup again and headed back to the cabin, hoping the water would warm enough to drink by the time she got there. She had already stretched out on the mattress by the time the other girls returned.

"Are you OK?" Darci bent over Helen and touched her forehead.

"Just tired," Helen replied. She felt a little dizzy, but she made herself sit up again.

As Ginger stretched out on her mattress she bumped her suitcase, and a small envelope fell off the top, its contents spilling on the floor.

Helen reached over and gathered up the small colorful squares.

"What beautiful stamps! All from Rwanda."

"Mrs. Layton gave me those," Ginger said, accepting the envelope from Helen.

"Do you collect stamps?"

Ginger nodded. "Do you?"

"Sure do. Started about two years ago when my family gave me a 'Traveler' stamp album. Last Christmas I got a 'Senior Statesman.' Boy, is it big. It wasn't much fun transferring all those stamps." Helen made a wry face. "But my father and I did it together. What's your favorite country?"

"I don't know." Ginger shrugged. "My aunt wants to work on them with me, but I just haven't felt like it." She paused. "Mom and I used to do them together."

Helen glanced down at her hands a moment, then smiled at the redhead. "Do you have the ones of the mask people from Liberia?"

Ginger smiled back. "Yeah, aren't they awful? My Mom said they gave her the creeps. But I like them." The two girls giggled at the thought of the grotesque stamps. "How about the dog series from Liberia?"

"I have those. And I have some horses and cars and lots of others."

"Quiet time," Darci called out. Reluctantly the girls began to settle down.

Helen felt even more tired and thirsty than before. Stretching out on the mattress, she fell into a troubled sleep and dreamed of stubborn horses, smelly skunks, and faces of witch doctors coming to life from her Liberian stamps. Only dimly did she realize that someone was placing a wet cloth on her head and holding a glass of cool orange juice to her lips. The sweet liquid did not quench her thirst. Her lips felt dry and cracked. Helen fell back into a restless sleep and dreamed of deserts and snakes and empty water coolers.

After quiet time the girls slipped out for surprise time, then returned to get ready for general line call and supper.

Helen slept on, rousing only slightly as the girls talked softly around her. She tried to remember what it was she needed to do, but the effort was too much, and she fell back into sleep.

By the time the girls returned from supper Darci greeted them with a cheerful "She's sleeping better. Probably just the heat and that sore ankle, not to mention all the excitement of getting ready to go home."

Marge wiped her wet forehead. "Today has certainly been a scorcher, that's for sure."

Tammy stayed with Helen while Darci escorted the girls to campfire.

In the soft darkness, the twins giggled and chirped as always. Dawn, Prissy, and Marge sat close together, watching the flames flicker and listening to the beautiful music as they welcomed in the

Sabbath. Ginger tossed small pebbles aimlessly to one side, fidgeted slightly, and then moved closer to Darci.

"May I go back to the cabin?"

"Campfire isn't over yet."

"I know. But I'm—I'm not a Seventh-day Adventist."

Darci sat thoughtfully a moment. "The Sabbath isn't just for Seventh-day Adventists, Ginger. It's God's gift to everyone. He made it long before the first Seventh-day Adventist was even born."

Ginger couldn't hold back a small grin. She tossed another pebble or two and then she turned back to Darci. "Why don't you people just go to church on Sunday like everyone else does?"

"Because Jesus gave us a beautiful gift when He made the world. It's called the Sabbath. It wouldn't be very polite to refuse a gift, would it?"

Ginger didn't answer, but her fidgeting ceased as Pastor Jack began to speak.

"I've been talking to you this week about standing up for what you believe. Tonight I'd like to tell you about someone very special who did just that. His name is Saddiq. Some of you may have already heard about him. Evangelist Joe Crews talks about him when he preaches. Saddiq is an East Indian. When he discovered Jesus he learned to love Him with all his heart. He even made the decision to be baptized and become a Seventh-day Adventist Christian. In his country Christians are considered traitors. Saddiq's family was taken away; he lost his job; his relatives tried to beat him to death. Even now he might be dead by the hands of a member of his own family. But he loved Jesus so much that he counted all that as nothing compared with his peace and joy in following Christ all the way. Some of you here tonight may not be committed Christians. You may be saying, 'But Saddiq is different. I couldn't do all that.' I don't think Saddiq could have, either, if he'd been thinking about himself. But the wonderful thing about Jesus is that when we take a good look at Him we stop looking at ourselves. Jesus helped Saddiq. He'll help you. If you give your heart to Him, He'll help you face anything."

Ginger turned to Darci. "Do you believe that?"

Darci nodded.

"Is it really true what Mrs. Layton said about Satan causing bad things to happen to try to make us not love Jesus, but that someday Jesus will have to destroy Satan and then there'll be no more bad things ever again?"

Darci nodded again. "Yes, that is true."

"My mamma never went to church. She didn't need Jesus, she said. But when she was dying she asked people to pray for her. And she sent me to live with a Christian. Why?"

"Because she realized that the loneliest thing in the world is not having Jesus."

Ginger glanced at Darci, and a tear tugged at her eyes. "Do you—do you think Jesus could forgive somebody who was as mad at Him as I was?"

Darci smiled as she gently touched the long red hair. "Yes, Ginger. He did a long time ago, on Calvary. He's just waiting for you to accept it."

The campers had finished the closing song, and Pastor Jack asked everyone to bow his head for prayer. Ginger clasped her hands together and struggled against the tears that threatened to engulf her.

* * *

Noises in the cabin made Helen open her eyes. The muffled voices of the girls and the darkness outside told her it was late.

"How are you feeling?" Marge and Dawn crowded around Helen as she turned to her side to watch them.

"OK, I guess. What time is it?"

"Time to go to sleep," Darci announced with a grin, and the girls, one by one, retired to their mattresses.

"I feel like I've already done a lot of that," Helen mumbled, but she closed her eyes and drifted into a restful and refreshing slumber. Darkness settled over the campers as crickets serenaded them.

Moonlight flooded the cabin as Ginger rose quietly from her bed and crossed to the counselors' mattresses. Touching Darci on the shoulder, she waited until the counselor sleepily sat up. "Did Jesus really cry when my mother died?"

"Yes, He did, Ginger," Darci whispered quietly. "I'm sure He did."

Ginger sat still for a moment, then turned around and just as quietly returned to her mattress.

Darci sat in the darkness, a quiet tear slipping unbidden down her cheek. "Thank You, Jesus," she whispered as she lay down again.

Helen turned over on her mattress and opened her eyes. In the light that filled the area by her bed she could see Ginger bent intently over a small book. I wonder what that girl is reading at this time of night, she thought drowsily. Straining to see, Helen could make out the print on the cover and with a pleased smile she drifted back to sleep. It was the first time, other than at group worship, that she had seen Ginger reading her Bible.

7

A Happy Day

Sabbath is a happy day, happy day, happy day." Helen hummed the kindergarten song as she dressed in her best clothes. She remembered how much fun she had helping her mom in the little children's Sabbath school class at home. I wonder how she'll do today without my help, Helen mused as she tucked in the last stray corner of her sheet and rose to join the others for morning devotional.

"You're not limping today and you don't look so pale," Marge commented after close scrutiny of her roommate. "Must be feeling better."

"Pretty good. Not ready to race anybody though," Helen added with a grin.

Outside small puffy clouds dotted the sky and gave promise of a slightly more tolerable day weatherwise. Helen walked leisurely behind the other girls from her unit as they made their way down the hill. Everyone was quiet and unusually subdued.

Breathing deeply of the cooler morning air, Helen walked slowly and listened for birds and small-animal sounds.

Breakfast in the tent went quickly, and then the girls gathered around the counselors. "Seems they have more visitors than they anticipated," Darci announced with a slight frown. "They need more chairs up at the worship site, and the pickup isn't available today."

"So each one of you needs to grab a chair and take it with you when you go up to worship after Sabbath school,'' Tammy added.

"The visitors are using the bus, so we'll be walking.'' Darci's mischievous grin returned.

"Oh, no,'' Dawn groaned as she glanced down at the new Sabbath shoes she was wearing.

"Told you those fancy things weren't very good for camp.'' Marge shook her head at her friend and added in a whisper, "I'll carry your chair; I have my old clunkers on.''

After the first part of Sabbath school the girls broke up into smaller groups for their classes. For their junior-age class, Marge, Ginger, and Helen went to one end of the cafeteria with the 10-year-olds from the other girls' cabins.

Ginger did not take part in the discussion of the lesson, but sat back listening to the animated conversation of the teacher and the other girls. Soon the teacher glanced at her watch and announced, "We have about ten more minutes and we've fairly well covered the lesson for this week. You've all studied very well, I'm pleased to see.'' She flashed a pleasant smile as she closed her quarterly and leaned back in her chair. "Are there any questions, not necessarily about this week's lesson, but just questions about something in general any of you would like to ask?''

After one or two girls had raised their hands and had their questions answered, Ginger slowly lifted hers.

"Yes, Ginger?'' The teacher's blue eyes sparkled as she leaned forward slightly.

Ginger awkwardly opened the Bible Darci had lent her only the Sunday before and turned to where a white ribbon marked a place. Pointing to the page, she asked, "Why does this person say, 'Our Father which art in heaven'? It's Jesus talking, isn't it?''

Mrs. Meadows glanced where Ginger pointed. "Yes. That's called the Lord's Prayer. Jesus was teaching the disciples how to pray.''

"Why does He say, 'Our Father'? Why didn't He just say, 'My Father'?''

73

Mrs. Meadows looked inquiringly at the class. "Would one of you like to answer Ginger's question?"

Sandy, from Unit Three, shot her hand up and waved it about.

"Yes, Sandy," Mrs. Meadows said, "you may answer the question."

"Because when we accept Jesus as our Saviour, He becomes our big brother. We're adopted into God's family. So God, who is Jesus' Father, becomes *our* Father, too." Sandy nodded as she finished.

"That's a very good answer, Sandy. We all become brothers and sisters in Christ. One big family, so to speak." Mrs. Meadows' smile crinkled her eyes.

Ginger glanced around at the other girls in her group. "So it's like having a whole bunch of sisters—you're all sisters!"

Sandy flashed her ready grin. "Yes, and since I'm an only kid, that's great news to me."

Ginger's gaze fell on the verse again. "And God is our—is our Father."

"Yes, Ginger," Mrs. Meadows said softly. "And the kindest, most loving Father you could ever want."

Ginger didn't answer, but let her hand rest on the page before her.

Just then the camp director sounded a hand bell, and the Sabbath school classes throughout the cafeteria began to break up.

Each of the girls folded her chair and carried it under one arm as they started out of the building and up the hill for worship hour.

Helen found herself setting hers down every few moments as she sighed wearily. "I didn't realize I was still tired," she muttered.

"Let me help you with that." Before Helen could speak Ginger had handed her the borrowed Bible, lifted the folded chair under her spare arm, and begun to trudge up the hill again. Helen blinked and followed along behind, pleasantly surprised.

When the girls topped the hill and came into the prepared clearing, Ginger set up the chairs side by side and accepted the Bible back. "Thanks, Ginger, I really appreciated that," Helen spoke gratefully.

Ginger shrugged, but a faint smile tugged at her lips.

One of the visiting pastors acted as guest speaker during the worship hour. Even though he was older and less enthusiastic in his presentation, Helen was pleased to see Ginger not only listening as closely as she had to Pastor Jack but following in her Bible the best she could. Occasionally Helen would help her locate one of the more difficult texts. Always the white-ribbon marker remained at Matthew 6, and Helen noticed that during the pauses in the service Ginger would flip back to her marker and reach out a finger to touch the page.

* * *

Prissy, Dawn, and Marge could hardly wait to introduce their families to everyone. As they all lined up for dinner Marge punched Helen in the ribs.

"I want to introduce my mother to the skinniest girl in the cabin." She grinned.

Helen smiled shyly at the attractive woman. She looked so different from the chubby, thrown-together appearance of her daughter.

"Now, Mom," Marge asked while a twinkle lighted her eyes, "do you really want me to be that skinny?"

Mrs. Mavis' smile grew wider as she turned to her daughter. "I'm sure Helen's mother doesn't think her a bit too slender."

"As a matter of fact, she says a good stiff wind would probably blow me away!"

"Is your mother here?" Marge stretched her neck this way and that.

Helen frowned slightly. "No, it's too far away to come for just a few hours. She'll be here tomorrow. You can meet her then." Helen grinned at her friend. "She's almost as skinny as I am!"

"Nobody is that thin except you!"

Dawn's loud "Hey, Gang!" caught Marge's and Helen's attention. Dragging her mother and father by the hand, she introduced them to Helen, who offered all three a place in the line in

75

front of her.

"No, thank you." Mrs. Dayton's voice was as soft and gentle as Dawn's was noisy and loud. "We'll take our places at the back. I don't think Dawn is starving to death."

Dawn groaned, but her mother smiled politely, and they hurried on down the line, Dawn's excited chatter floating back to Helen.

"I haven't seen the twins' parents, have you, Marge?"

Marge shook her head. "No, but I know they were supposed to come." A quick glance up and down the line did not locate either the twins or their family.

"Maybe they're already inside." Helen took her tray as the line entered the shelter of the cook's garage. The food smelled unusually good, and Helen eagerly pointed to several of the containers, indicating her choices to the server.

Mrs. Mavis' smile broadened as she followed Helen to the tent. "How *do* you stay so slender with an appetite like that?"

"She throws most of it away," Marge interrupted. "She's not only skinny but she's also a picky eater!"

But Helen was to prove Marge wrong this time. She cleaned her plate and returned to the line for seconds before Marge had half finished her own tray of food.

"There are the twins over there." Helen pointed to a table to the far right as she returned to her place next to Marge.

"I don't see their parents, do you?"

Helen shook her head as she chewed a big mouthful of food. Swallowing at last, she muttered, "Just Darci and Tammy are with them. I wonder if anything is wrong?"

Marge shrugged her shoulders. Just then Helen saw Ginger moving back down the aisle between the tables, her tray empty. A lonely look in her eyes made Helen remember something.

"I wonder whether Ginger's aunt is here."

Again Marge shrugged and turned back to her food.

No one followed Ginger from the tent as she stacked her tray and prepared to leave.

"Helen?" The counselor's voice startled her as she sat watching Ginger's retreating back. "I was wondering whether you'd like to join the twins and me on a nature walk—unless you have plans."

Helen shook her head. "No plans. There isn't anything scheduled for the campers this afternoon?"

Darci shook her head. "Not for a while. Most of the boys and girls will be showing their families around, then we'll be getting back together for vespers and campfire later. Excuse me, I'm going to see if Ginger wants to go too," Darci added hurriedly as she glanced after Ginger.

Helen watched Darci dart out of the tent. "I guess Ginger's aunt didn't make it today either."

"Huh?" Marge turned to Helen, a puzzled look on her face.

"Nothing—I'm going with Darci on a nature walk. Guess I'll see you at supper later."

"Wouldn't miss it." Marge's smile reached from ear to ear.

As Helen collected her empty dishes and stacked them on her tray before leaving she could hear Mrs. Mavis' friendly laugh. "I thought you said she was picky!"

Marge just shook her head. "I never know what to think about her."

Helen scrambled up the hill to the cabin. Ginger and Darci were talking quietly as she entered. From her suitcase Helen pulled out her jeans, tennis shoes, and shirt. As she changed she could hear Darci's voice trying to persuade Ginger to go on the walk with them.

"—the twins' parents couldn't make it today after all. I thought it might help cheer them up if we go hunting for unusual rocks and things the way they like to do. You don't have to go, but I thought you might enjoy it too. We'll be going down where that creek is, the one with the grapevine swing."

Silence filled the outer room as Helen buckled her belt and slipped on her shoes. Suddenly she called out, "I'll show you our climbing hill, where I camped with my family. And a neat little waterfall, if you'd like me to." By now she had finished tying her shoes and joined Darci and Ginger in the front room.

Ginger studied first Darci, then Helen. "OK, I'll go." Standing up, she headed for her suitcase and began to change clothes.

Darci stood too, and patted Helen's shoulder. Her lips formed the word Thanks, and Helen blushed. "I'm going to get Tammy and the twins. Be back in a jif," Darci called out as she headed out the door.

Helen sat in silence while Ginger finished changing. While they waited in the outer room for the twins and the counselors, Helen began to tell Ginger about her family's vacation the summer before.

"We even went hiking in the Smokies. I didn't think we'd ever get to the top of the mountain we were climbing. I think my father said it was about 6,000 feet high. Do you like to hike, Ginger?"

Ginger shrugged. "Mom and I went camping a few times, but she wasn't much for mountain climbing. We'd go for long walks and talk though. It was kind of nice."

The twins' giggles could be heard outside as they neared the cabin. They burst like rockets into the room where Ginger and Helen sat, and raced for their suitcases in the back room where they eagerly changed into hiking clothes.

"I hope we find something really great today!" Lucy called out as she tugged on her jeans.

"I wouldn't mind seeing some neat birds." Darci pulled out her binoculars and bird book.

"I'll settle for just not getting blisters." Tammy rubbed the back of her foot where her new Sabbath shoes had begun to irritate the heel. Slipping on her beat-up sneakers, she let out a sigh. "I always was a country girl at heart."

Before long the small group left the cabin and headed up the hill.

"Look at the difference!" Helen could hardly believe how much work had been done on the old cabin since their move down the hill. It now had a completed interior, doors, and windows, and was a twin to their cabin down the hill.

After a brief inspection of the improvements, they entered the wooded area behind the cabins and followed Tammy, who was most familiar with all the back trails, until they could hear the sound of water up ahead.

Breaking out of the brush and undergrowth, the girls climbed down a slight embankment and followed the creek until they came to the clearing where abandoned campsites stood as evidence of the many uses campers had made of the area.

The counselors sat on a large, flat boulder and, gathering the four girls around, read a few pages to them from the book Darci had been using for her daily personal devotions. After a brief prayer, Darci spoke first.

"What would you like to do? Any specifics?"

"Collect rocks!" piped up the twins. Lucy was already examining the ground around her for a good find.

Ginger wrinkled her nose, and Tammy spoke up. "How about bird watching? After all, we do have a bird nut here."

Darci grinned. "I just happen to have my bird book along if anyone is interested."

"I'd like to show Ginger the waterfall I found last summer!" It was Helen's first contribution to the conversation.

As each girl continued to make her suggestions, Tammy raised a hand. "I have an idea"—glancing at her watch she motioned to Helen—"you have a watch on, and so does Darci. I have mine. Let's all go do what we'd like for an hour, then meet back here, and we'll do some exploring or something together. How does that sound?"

The girls voiced their agreement, and Tammy offered to take the twins rock hunting since they had no watch.

Darci eagerly set off alone with her bird book and Helen and Ginger started off together.

"There is a trail, sort of, right along the edge of this dirt wall, between it and the creek. If we follow it we'll see the waterfall and the diving hole."

Ginger made her way carefully behind Helen. After a time they came to a barbed-wire fence.

"We can't go any farther!" Ginger stood staring at the barrier.

"Sure we can." Helen carefully held up a section of the barbed wire with one hand while she pressed the lower strand down with a foot. With a little effort the slender redhead was through and on the other side. "It won't hurt if you're careful," Helen reassured Ginger, who now repeated the process, allowing Helen to squeeze through the fence. Soon they made their way down another embankment, and there before them was Helen's waterfall. Small, but beautiful, a natural setback in the dirt-and-rock wall surrounded a small pool area that joined the creek. Water cascaded down the wall opposite the girls.

Helen sat down on a natural ledge and began to toss small leaves and twigs into the water. They whirled about before floating off toward the main creek.

The twittering of birds mingled with the sound of rushing water to fill the comfortable silence that surrounded the two girls.

After some time they stood up and began to follow the path back along the creek's edge.

"I wonder whether any of those stones are sharp?" Ginger stopped and examined the bed of rocks they could see through the clear-flowing water.

"No, not very. Mostly slippery." Helen paused and eyed Ginger. "Would you like to wade?"

Ginger smiled back at Helen. "I haven't waded in ages. Sure, let's."

So they carefully tied their tennis shoes together and tucked their socks into their shoes. Then they rolled up their pant legs and cautiously stepped out into the cool water.

Ginger began to giggle as the water rushed past her ankles. "I feel like a little kid."

After several yards Helen pointed to a spot just ahead, where several large rocks jutted out from the right side of the creekbank. "That's the diving hole. It was really deep when we were here last year, but the water is so low this year I'm sure there's not much water in there, either."

Ginger inched closer to the drop-off. The water, though obviously down quite a bit, still appeared quite deep.

As they moved on past the drop-off Helen commented, ''We saw a few snakes there too when we were here before.''

Ginger turned pale and waded even faster until she was safely past the large rocks. ''Aren't you scared of snakes?''

Helen shrugged. ''Sometimes. My father said most snakes are harmless. If you see enough of them it gets so they don't bother you too much.'' Remembering the night visitor they had had at the cabin earlier in the week, she blushed and grinned. ''I *don't* like snakes at nighttime; I'm always afraid of stepping on them. Yuck!''

Wading side by side, the girls soon returned to where they were to meet the rest of the hikers. ''We still have lots of time. Let's go climb the hill,'' Helen said.

Struggling up the creek embankment, the girls dried their feet on the grass and tugged on their socks and shoes.

''Where's the hill?'' Ginger stood up and studied the area.

Helen blushed again. ''It's right here.'' She motioned to a rather sharp incline that led to an upper level of pasture area. Then she explained. ''My brothers and I used to call it our mountain until we went to the Smokies and saw *real* mountains.''

The girls struggled up the incline, laughing happily as they slid part of the way back down on their stomachs only to regain their footing and try again.

''My dad can get up it easy.'' Helen panted from the exercise as she sat at the top overlooking their meeting point. They relaxed, partially hidden by shrubbery, and were about to return to the clearing when they heard voices below.

Motioning for Ginger to be quiet, Helen whispered something in her ear. The two girls flattened out on their stomachs and smothered their giggles while the counselors and the twins gathered in the area below them.

''It's been an hour; they should be back soon.'' Tammy glanced at her watch and then toward the trail.

"I hope they didn't get lost." Lucy's voice sounded concerned, and her eyes grew wider as she stared at her sister.

"I don't think they did. Probably just not noticing the time." Darci flipped through her book and showed Tammy a picture of a bird she had seen on her walk. "They're not too common around here," she added proudly.

"What was that?" Susie looked around, startled, as a small shower of pebbles landed just in front of her feet.

"Don't know." Tammy glanced back, but seeing nothing unusual, turned back to Lucy. "Show Darci the rocks and fossils we found."

Just as Lucy began to unwrap the handkerchief she held, another shower of small pebbles clattered down around the girls, who now craned their necks backward as they looked toward the clear-blue sky.

"Never heard of it raining pebbles before," Darci laughed.

"Maybe the sky is falling," Lucy and Susie giggled.

Helen and Ginger, about to burst with repressed laughter, rolled toward the edge of the embankment and slid down the incline on their seats, landing with a solid thud a short distance from the startled girls.

Darci, the first to recover from the surprise, solemnly held out a hand to Ginger and Helen and smiled. "So nice of you to drop in. Do come and see us again sometime."

* * *

"Look at all the people," Helen whispered to Tammy as they found places at the campfire later that evening.

"With all the visitors it sure makes a nice crowd. Ought to be able to hear us sing clear to Austin."

Debbie seemed extra lively as she bounced to the center of the clearing. "Hasn't this been a great Sabbath?" Without waiting for an answer she began to strum on her guitar. "Let's start off tonight with 'Jesus Is the Sweetest Name I Know.' I think everyone here is familiar with it and I really expect to hear some good singing with a fine group like this."

Voices flooded the clearing and spread like a beautiful blanket of melody over the ranch. The stillness of the night caught the tunes and spread them out, over, and around the hills and trees.

Song after song poured into the night until Debbie held up a hand for quiet. "For our last song I'd like us to sing 'Oh, Friend, Do You Love Jesus?' and everyone on this side"—motioning to those seated to her right—"will sing the first part. Everyone on this side"—now motioning to the left—"will sing the second part."

" 'Oh, friend, do you love Jesus?' " rang out from the right side.

Helen, on the left, joined in answering, " 'Oh, yes, I love Jesus.' "

Again the right side sang out, " 'Are you sure you love Jesus?' "

" 'I'm sure I love Jesus' " was the musical answer.

Back to the right, " 'And why do you love Jesus?' "

" 'Here's why I love Jesus.' "

All the voices joined together, " 'Because He first loved me.' "

" 'That's the reason we all ought to love Him,' " Debbie sang out.

" 'Oh, how I love Jesus,
Oh, how I love Jesus,
Oh, how I love Jesus,
Because He first loved me.' "

As the last note trailed off into the night Debbie slipped from the clearing, and Pastor Jack, tall, dark-skinned, Bible held firmly in hand, strode forward.

All eyes focused on him as he stood motionless. Bowing his head, he prayed, "Dear Father in heaven, help us truly to love Your Son, who so freely shed His blood that we, through Him, might live. In Jesus' name. Amen." Pastor Jack gazed in silence at the faces half hidden by the darkness. The firelight cast its shadows across the still circle. *"Do* you love Jesus?" A deep silence fell over the circle as the pastor paused. "Do you love Jesus?" Pastor Jack relaxed his shoulders as he rested his right hand on the Bible he held before him. "This book represents our closest connection with Heaven. In it are

words of life—beautiful, wonderful, important words. In this book is
told the story of a Man, a special Man, called the Christ.''

Pastor Jack quickly painted a word picture of the sacrifice of
Jesus, beginning with the promise of a Messiah to Adam and Eve in
the Garden of Eden and carrying his listeners down through the ages,
until they stood by the Mount watching Christ ascending into the
clouds. ''Soon, very soon, we all hope, we will look into the sky one
night''—here Pastor Jack raised a hand to the starry heavens above as
every gaze followed his—''and there we will see the most dazzling
scene ever to unfold before man's view! We will see Christ, not as a
servant or a sacrifice, but as a king, surrounded by thousands upon
thousands of brilliant beings, encircled by the wonderful rainbow of
promise, and wearing on His head the victor's crown. We will see it
all, not with our imagination, but with our eyes; not just as a hope, but
as a reality. And Christ will call us to Him. Then the angels will carry
us through the sky to join our Saviour in the most impressive
triumphal parade ever to be witnessed by the universe, as we return
with Him to New Jerusalem, that city of indescribable beauty beyond
our comprehension. Never more will tears be shed, or hopes crushed,
or life be cut short. No more sickness, or war or——'' Pastor Jack
lowered his gaze once more to those before him. ''I want to see Jesus
face to face. I want to be part of that triumphal procession entering
New Jerusalem. I want to see God and to know Him as He knows
me—do *you?*''

Helen felt something deep within her tugging at her heart in the
hush that deepened around the campfire. Even though she was
already baptized, she felt there was something more Jesus wanted her
to do now.

''How many of you young people tonight would like to dedicate
yourself completely to preparing yourself for the Lord's return. How
many of you want to say with me, 'Lord, help me do what I can to
bring that wonderful time of Your appearing that much closer'? If you
would like to take that stand for Jesus please rise.''

Helen now knew what God wanted of her. Slowly she rose to her feet, shoulders erect, head held high, her eyes fixed on the earnest face of Pastor Jack. "I want to be like Jesus. I want to love Jesus always. I want Him to come soon," she whispered in her heart.

"Thank you, every one of you, for having the courage to make that kind of commitment." Pastor Jack bowed his head. "Dear God in heaven, bless each one here tonight that we might all be drawn closer to You in the days and weeks ahead. I pray You will be with those who stood in commitment to You. Strengthen them, draw them onward, help them never to settle for less than their best, and may they hold fast to the promise of Your soon return, no matter how difficult the way may seem. In Jesus' name we pray. Amen."

Through tears Helen gazed at Debbie, who now stood in the clearing in the pastor's place. Guitar in hand, she spoke quietly, "Let's all stand and join hands as far as possible while we close with 'Side by Side.' "

" 'Side by side we stand awaiting God's command,
Worshiping the saving King.
Living by His grace and moving on in faith;
Jesus Himself will see us through.
Meet me in heaven, we'll join hands together;
Meet me by the Saviour's side.
I'll meet you in heaven, we'll sing songs together;
Brothers and sisters, I'll be there!
Soldiers all are we to go where Jesus leads,
We'll fight in faith and we will overcome.
Heaven is our goal, and saving every soul;
Pray that we all will be there.' "

As the chorus rang out the second time, movement at the far side of the circle caught Helen's attention and her heart seemed to leap as she smiled through her tears. Before she could motion for Tammy to look, two figures had joined a third taller one and slipped beyond the crowd into the darkness. Had Tammy seen it? Helen glanced at the counselor, but Tammy's eyes were fastened on Debbie.

Vibrating with joy, Helen's voice again rang out, " 'I'll meet you

85

in heaven, we'll sing songs together; Brothers and sisters, I'll be there! . . . Pray that we all will be there.' "

As the circle of campers and visitors broke up and folks made their way back to the cabins and waiting cars, Helen's eyes quickly searched the area behind the clearing. There, with one hand resting reassuringly on the shoulder of a teary-faced redheaded girl, sat Pastor Jack and Mrs. Layton.

"It was Ginger and Mrs. Layton I saw go up to Pastor Jack during the song—it really was." Helen almost skipped down the hill. "Maybe, just maybe——" Hardly daring to voice her hope, she chewed on her lower lip absentmindedly. "Dear Jesus, I do hope Ginger *has* decided to love You. Oh, *please* may she love You."

8
Goodbyes

Good morning to you, good morning to you, good morning, Tammy and Darci, good morning to you.''

The counselors stirred sleepily and sat up, rubbing their eyes. There, gathered around them, stood their girls. The twins' eyes twinkled as they hopped up and down. Marge and Dawn were less bouncy, but obviously pleased with themselves about something. Helen's eyes sparkled with some gentle mischief, and Prissy, no longer shy and retiring, but very much a part of the gang, grinned happily. Ginger sat on the end of her mattress, a smile lighting her face.

"What is all this about?" Tammy tried to sound indignant. "Don't you know *we're* supposed to wake you sleepyheads up? Not the other way around!"

The twins giggled, and Lucy, no longer able to hold back the secret, stepped forward and offered the counselors a bulky item wrapped in a bright-yellow handkerchief. "We didn't have any wrapping paper," she apologized and giggled again.

Tammy's dark eyes widened as she accepted the gift. When she untied the single knot the corners of the handkerchief fell back to reveal several beautifully colored stones the girls had collected on their nature walks during the week. Picking up one fossil that she recognized, Tammy grinned. "And to think that you girls made me help gather my own gift!"

The twins smothered their giggles with their hands and tried to hide the blush that crept over their light freckles. Helen then stepped forward and handed Darci something wrapped in an identical yellow handkerchief.

Darci's mouth fell open as she held up the unusual snail shell Helen had found earlier in the week. "Helen, it's your fossil! Are you sure you want to part with it?"

Helen's face reddened, and she dropped her gaze to the wood floor. "It's to say Thank you for being so nice to me that day I was sick."

"Hey, I was nice to you too," Tammy protested playfully. "It's true, though, Darci did take care of you while I went to dinner. A sacrifice like that deserves recognition." Tammy punched her chubbier roommate in the ribs as she winked at Helen.

Prissy held out two gifts, one in each hand, and presented them to both counselors at the same time.

"Prissy, how beautiful!" Tammy held up a delicate water color, about six by eight inches, framed in natural wood.

"It's our cabin." Dawn reached out a finger to touch the frame. "Did you get the wood for the frame from around here?"

Prissy nodded, and her eyes glowed.

"I didn't know you could paint," Darci exclaimed as she held up her gift, a picture about the same size as Tammy's.

"Why, that's Dandy!" Helen's eyes widened as she gazed at the almost lifelike painting of the big black-and-brown horse.

"They're great!" All the girls ohed and ahed over the pictures.

"So that was your big secret at crafts," murmured Susie as she and Lucy admired one of the paintings that sat propped on Darci's extra suitcase by the front door.

"I've always wanted to paint"—Prissy's cheeks had turned a bright red—"but Mom said it was too messy. Anyway, they let me do those in crafts this week."

"Prissy, these are wonderful! I want your mother to see them." And with that Darci carefully rearranged the suitcase and pictures

88

where anyone entering the cabin couldn't help seeing them. "With talent like that, your mom *has* to let you paint."

I wonder whether anyone has ever praised Prissy for anything before, Helen thought, smiling at the girl, whose sparkling eyes and brightened cheeks made her glow. She's certainly not an awkward baby anymore. Her mom won't even recognize her.

"With all these fancy presents, ours don't seem so great anymore," Dawn whispered to Marge.

Marge took two small, flat, rectangular items from behind Dawn's back, where she had hidden them, and strode over to the counselors. "They're not as big and bulky as everybody else's presents," she began in her dry manner, "but we were trying to be considerate—we didn't want to clutter up your suitcases too much." Helen playfully punched Marge in the ribs, and the chubby girl let out a yelp. "Save me! I'm being attacked by the skinny people!" With that, Dawn, Prissy, and the twins all began to tickle and poke Marge until she gasped out "Uncle."

Darci and Tammy chuckled at the cards the two girls had made for them. "You didn't even have to sign it, Marge," Darci said with a grin. "It *sounds* just like you."

Everyone else crowded around the counselors while they read aloud: " 'I'd like to tell you what a great time I had and how much I enjoyed myself' "—Darci flipped to the inside of the card—" 'but my mother taught me not to fib.' "

"Listen to this one," Tammy said as she began to read her card. " 'Has anyone ever told you how good-looking, kind, and generous you are?' " Flipping her card open, Tammy continued, " 'You didn't *really* believe them, did you?' "

"Actually, you two are the best counselors and this is the best camp I have ever been to," Marge said seriously, then darted back into the girls' bedroom.

A tear tugged at the corner of Darci's eyes. "Thanks. You've all been a pretty nice bunch yourselves."

The older girls carefully rewrapped their gifts before storing them in their suitcases, but found themselves still yawning sleepily. Tammy picked up her watch. "Hey, you clowns," she protested, "do you know what time it is?"

Several heads appeared in the doorway. "No!" they called out together.

"It's 5:30 A.M.! We don't have to be up for another hour!" All the heads disappeared again as Tammy flung a pillow in their direction.

"Oh, well," Darci called out cheerily, "since we're all awake we might as well give the cabin one last good cleaning."

A chorus of groans exploded from the back room, followed by several thuds as the girls dived for their beds. Instantly all was quiet, with only two or three loud snores here and there.

Darci, stretching out on her bed, tucked her hands behind her head. "That ought to keep 'em quiet for a while." A few minutes later she opened her eyes again to see Ginger standing by the side of her mattress holding out the Bible she had been using all week. "I—I don't have a present, but I wanted to return this and say thanks—to both of you—for everything."

Darci eased herself to a sitting position and accepted the offered Bible. Then she reached into her suitcase. "When I got ready to pack for camp something told me to bring this extra Bible with me. It's a special gift edition I had planned to use for a Christmas present. But I think the Lord wanted me to bring it to camp and give it to you. It's a little early, but Merry Christmas, if you'd like it."

Ginger hesitated only a moment before extending her hand to accept the white leather book. Tracing the gold lettering on its cover, she carefully opened it to the marker. "I've never owned a Bible before," she said softly.

"There's a place in front that says 'Presented by ———.' Would it be OK if I sign it for you as a gift from me?"

Ginger returned the Bible to Darci, who carefully filled in the information on the flyleaf. "May I have Tammy sign it too?" she asked, pen still in hand.

"Sure, if she'd like to."

Tammy reached out quickly. "Sure I would."

Ginger held the Bible close to her heart and smiled warmly at the counselors as she returned to her mattress.

Helen turned to face the redheaded girl, whom she now counted as a friend. "I'm glad you came to camp, Ginger—I really am!"

Ginger gazed at her mattress, a faint reddish glow brightening her cheeks.

"So am I, Ginger. I mean it!" Marge added quickly.

One by one the other girls chimed in until tears started at the corner of Ginger's eyes.

"OK, guys, time to rise and shine," Darci called out at just the right moment. She clapped her hands and grinned broadly. "No breakfast until this cabin is spotless!"

"Oh, no!" Again the groans went up, but Tammy ignored the protests and began calling out names and jobs until everyone was racing around dusting, sweeping, and cleaning.

Before the campers had finished breakfast, cars were piling into the clearing, and parents, eager to pick up their youngsters, headed this way and that.

"Is your mom here yet?" Marge asked breathlessly, as she lugged her oversize suitcase out to the waiting car. Taking the luggage from his daughter, Mr. Mavis flashed Helen a warm smile, then heaved the suitcase into the trunk.

"Not yet. I guess you don't get to meet her after all. But I'll send you a picture of my family sometime if you'll write to me." Hastily exchanging addresses, the two girls said their goodbyes and parted. Marge waved from the back window until the car turned a corner.

Hands shoved deep into her jeans pockets, Helen stood in the clearing staring down the road. One by one her fellow campers departed. Waving first to Dawn, and then to the twins, as they pulled out of sight, Helen began to fidget and pace. Suddenly she stiffened and began to jump up and down, waving her arms. "Mom! Dad!" She raced across the clearing, barely allowing the blue station wagon time to stop before she jerked open its doors.

Helen's three brothers and younger sister poured out of the car. There was much hugging and kissing as everybody talked at once.

"Hey, gang, I've only been gone a week!" Helen laughed and then struggled free to fly to her mother and father.

"You've only been gone a week, remember?" Father playfully scolded as he hugged his older daughter to him.

"I just have to finish packing and I'm all set. We've changed cabins. This one is really nice. We had a skunk visit us and a bull and a snake!" Helen chattered excitedly as she led her family to the cabin.

"Can we explore?" Joe piped up as they reached Helen's cabin.

Mother nodded approval. "But stay right around here so we can find you when it's time to go."

Helen showed her parents around the half-empty cabin, showing off the improvements. Then she knelt by her mattress to finish packing. Suddenly a loud war whoop almost by her ear made Helen jump.

"What in the world?" Darci, who had just entered the cabin, almost dropped her armload of gear. Popping into the back room to investigate, she saw Helen toss a piece of wadded-up paper at the open window. "Just my silly brothers playing spy or something!"

"Look what I found!" Timmy held up a long cord, at the end of which dangled a small, black rectangular object.

"My camera!" Helen gasped. "Where was it?"

"Right here." Timmy motioned beneath the window where the boys were playing.

"I thought I laid it up there. It must have gotten knocked off." Helen reached through the window and took hold of the cord. "I sure hope it still works. Wait till I write to Marge. Boy, will I have news for her!"

"I'm glad you found it." Ginger entered the back room and sat down on the mattress beside her packed suitcase.

Helen blushed as she remembered the suspicion that had surrounded Ginger after the disappearance of the camera. "I'm glad too, *very* glad."

A noise in the outer room caught Helen's attention as she snapped the suitcase shut. Darci stood by the front door holding up the two paintings. "Prissy did these, Mrs. Thompson. Aren't they good?"

The newcomer's mouth dropped open. *"My* little Prissy did these?"

"Yes, ma'am, she sure did!"

"You should see all the nice things we made in crafts, and I'm learning to ride. I can even get up on a horse all by myself—all sorts of things." Prissy glowed as she bounced up and down beside her parents.

"See, Hazel, I told you Prissy isn't a baby. Pastor Ben was right; camp has been a good experience for her." Mr. Thompson reached out a large hand and rumpled Prissy's hair.

Mrs. Thompson stood speechless, and Prissy rushed on. "Can I take art lessons now, Mamma? Can I? I promise not to make a mess. I'll put paper on the floor and everything!" She stopped bouncing and stood erect, scarcely breathing, her eyes never leaving her mother's face, her hands clasped together.

Mr. Thompson cleared his throat. "I don't see any reason why you shouldn't take art lessons." He admired first one picture, then the other, lingering over the one of Dandy. "Always wanted to be an artist myself, Hazel. I can't see any reason why she shouldn't have those lessons. Can you?" His eyebrows knitted together sternly, and Mrs. Thompson simply shook her head.

"No, dear, no reason at all," she answered meekly.

Prissy's cheeks glowed as she lugged the suitcase out the cabin door. "I can do it, Mamma." She ignored her mother's protests. "I'm a big girl now!"

Mr. Thompson tossed Darci a warm grin. "Thank you, young lady. You don't know how much I appreciate this."

The two counselors, who were watching the small Prissy dragging out her huge suitcase, shared a chuckle as the girl's excited voice filtered back to them.

"I'll take this one down to the car." Helen's father carted the suitcase out the door while Mother left to collect the rest of the children.

Helen stood by her mattress, her hands tucked into her jeans pockets. "May I write to you sometime, Ginger?"

Ginger nodded. She wrote her address on a slip of paper and handed it to Helen. "I'd like that."

"Do you think you'll be back to NVR next year?"

Ginger shrugged. "It's up to my aunt, I guess, but I think I'd like to come back."

"If I'm here, too, maybe we can go hiking again." Peeking into the other room, Helen added, a bit more loudly, "We might even drop in on some counselors again."

Ginger laughed. It was a soft, gentle laugh that brought a twinkle to her green eyes. "That's a deal!"

Turning to leave, Helen hesitated. "Goodbye, friend."

Ginger blushed. "Don't forget to write."

Helen shook her head. "I won't forget. Maybe we can even trade stamps or something."

Ginger nodded.

Helen said goodbye to Darci and Tammy and started down the hill. As she reached the clearing she passed an older woman with graying hair and a worried look. Helen smiled shyly. The woman's smile was gentle and lit up her face before the worried look returned. At the station wagon she glanced back to see the woman headed toward their cabin. I guess that is Ginger's aunt. She looks as though she'd make a good mother. Helen smiled to herself and climbed into the seat with her brothers and sister.

As the blue station wagon turned around in the clearing Helen glanced back over her shoulder. She saw Ginger, suitcase in hand, walking with the gentle-looking gray-haired lady. As the older woman rested one hand on the girl's shoulder and spoke to her, Ginger lifted her gaze to meet her aunt's and nodded. Helen thought she could see a smile on her face.

Joe tugged at his sister's shirt sleeve. "I said, what was your favorite part of camp?"

Helen settled into the seat and took a deep breath. She remembered the horses and the campfires, the skunks and the adventures, even the disappointments and being sick. Then she thought about Ginger and smiled. "I guess I liked it all, really, but the best part—the very best part—was winning a friend."

Tossing up dust clouds, the blue station wagon made its way safely down the hill. It turned right at the main ranch road, pulled out onto the highway just past the "Nameless Valley Ranch" marker, and turned left, heading for home. The first week of camp, for Nameless Valley Ranch and for Helen Brown, was over.